Dear Sister

Dear Sister

There's Something Black Women Want You to Know

PAULA DANNIELLE

Dear Sister: There's Something Black Women Want You to Know

Published by LIS'N, LLC
Charlotte, North Carolina

Paperback ISBN: 979-8-9887725-0-7
eBook ISBN: 979-8-9887725-1-4

Author: Paula Dannielle
Editing Team: Lauren Sellers and Jessica Hatmaker
Cover and Insert Design: Sara Wasserboehr
Interior Design: Robert Kern, TIPS Publishing Services, Carrboro, North Carolina

First Printing, July 2023

Dedication

Dear my only full-blood sister,
Michelle,
You are loved.
You are missed.
But I'm glad you are now whole.

Contents

Preface

In 1992, Whitney Houston repeated Chaka Khan's sentiment and reminded us that whatever the world needs, women have a natural inclination to provide it. In 1995, Gwen Stefani reminded the world that as a woman, you will never be "just a girl" and that we can strike out past societal limitations. In 2011, Beyoncé reminded us that girls run the world. Women have a strange relationship with society. The world knows it cannot function without us, yet it still seems to attempt to silence our contributions.

History would like to quiet the contributions of women coming together to create pathways and hideaways for melanated people escaping the horrors of American slavery. Society wants to try to minimize our influence on politics. However, any historian will tell you that Eleanor Roosevelt had just as much to do with helping America progress through the Great Depression as Franklin Delano. War tales would have us believe that women don't impact world relations. Still, six million women worked in factories in the United States, and hundreds of thousands served in militaristic roles during World War II. Or even that our activity in the Civil Rights Movement began and ended with Mrs. Rosa Parks taking a seat on the bus, when in reality, we organized sit-ins, printed leaflets, were on the front lines of marches, and gave speeches too! Our strength to impact the world is unparalleled.

Maybe that is why invisible and, let's be honest, visible powers fight so hard against us coming together.

While women can level the highest of mountains when we come together, history is also full of examples of the ugliness that emerges when we feud against each other. As far back as Genesis (*yes, I'm a preacher, so let's establish early on that while this is not necessarily a book for only Christians, there's a lot of Bible in this book*), Sarai was jealous of Hagar even though her hatred was a result of her own ill-devised plans. In First Samuel 1, Hannah had her husband's heart but Peninnah, Elkanah's other wife, had his children. Peninnah was so jealous of Elkanah's love for Hannah that she tormented her relentlessly, driving Hannah to the point of intoxicated prayer. And when a mother in First Kings 3 realizes her baby has died in the middle of the night, in a fit of jealousy and grief, she steals another woman's baby and tries to pass it off as her own. While these women were feuding, other women were working together to influence history in a positive direction.

When left without the protection of husbands, fathers, or sons, Naomi and Ruth worked together to ensure each other's survival in a patriarchal world. Elizabeth, the mother of John the Baptist, and Mary, the mother of Jesus, came together at a critical point in history to support each other during geriatric and unwed pregnancies. And if you ask the writer of the Gospel of Mark, three women went to the tomb, supporting each other in grief and ritual, only to find a risen Jesus so they could return and deliver the message to the hiding male disciples. In Biblical, ancient, and current history, the influence of women is at every turn. Indeed, women run the world.

And with that kind of power and influence, it begs the question, where are we taking it? Are we moving the future direction of the world toward good or evil? Are we furthering causes for justice or oppression? Are we working to establish God's

Kingdom here on earth, or are we out to seek power for ourselves regardless of how it hurts anyone else? Are we lying as victims in our inherited sin, or are we leading and serving as instruments to heal humanity? Are we moving the world forward?

This book is my attempt to contribute to helping us, Black women and non-Black women, move the world forward. In moving the world forward, sometimes it is as simple as addressing what is holding your community captive. But for me, and thanks to the history of the United States, moving the world forward for women is no simple matter. Our forward movement toward civility, justice, and equality has canyons of racism, classism, and sexism that have kept us from coming together. While the early European colonizers established race as another variable to excuse horrific acts of oppression, women also had to fight against sexism and chauvinism. And when the attributes of Black and female intersected, Black women found themselves as the recipients of double oppression.

Men silenced our voices because we were women. White women silenced our voices because we were Black. White men had the upper hand because they were white and male. White women had their skin. And where society stole so much from Black men, they still had the male privilege to work for them. Black women, well, let's just say, society has repeatedly tried to drown out who we are and what we contribute. But those exact efforts continue to put us at the center of the conversation.

Black women sit at the unique intersectionality of racism and sexism. We experience injustice from all sides and thus have the best vantage point to help society get to a better world tomorrow by continuing to address and dismantle the horrors that led us to today. If our world will ever experience equality, we must be willing to hear the stories of those suffering from unequal treatment. If we want a more just society, we must be willing to learn from those who have been dealt with unjustly. And if we want reconciled communities, each of our communities must be willing to listen to the ones who are constantly placed on the outside. If we, women, are going to move our world forward, we have to be willing to listen and learn from the experiences of Black women.

While conversations are emotionally costly, if "conversation is the currency of change,"[1] we must continue to be willing to spend it. That's why during 2021 and 2022, I surveyed Black women–the "Sistahs"–from all over the United States, across different geographic regions, educational levels, and economic classes to discover what topics Black women felt White women–the "Sisters"–needed to know. There were things Black women needed to continue to say and things that White women needed to hear.

While the answers to the surveys varied, most came down to nine things that Black women wish White women knew and they were tired of discussing. We took months to do interviews, collect surveys, and analyze data to take their responses and shape them into letters. This book is the result of the raw comments from those surveys, historical data, and my heartfelt experiences constructed into letters to White women, our Sisters.

While the data leans into my research background, and the Biblical passages are a natural flow out of my pastoral work, please also know that these letters are personal. I am a part of the community of which I speak. I am a Black woman raised in majority White spaces. I attended White schools and predominantly White universities. And while the richness of the African American church tradition developed my faith and affirmed my vocation, I currently serve at a predominantly White evangelical southern congregation.

I have been hurt by White women I've called friends when I realized they loved the part of me that assimilated into their culture without them ever having to understand mine. I also have

White Sisters who have been on this journey of racial reconciliation. They've read the books, researched the history, and then came to me for current context and application of the information they had gathered. As they've found the courage to look into the racist history of this nation that they have benefited from, they also found the strength to fight for women of all races as well.

While America continues to find unique ways to stifle the experiences and voices of Black women, those relationships with White women that were doing the work of dismantling racism confirmed for me that when we build sisterhood together, the world is better for us all. I have first-hand experience with the pain of racial injustice as well as the healing that can come from relationships with people on their own journey of reconciliation.

The phrasing in this work is intentional. First, throughout this book, you will read the term "Black" rather than "African American." This book is about the impact of race, not nationality or ethnicity. A person can be racialized as Black, and not be African, American, or African American. Traditionally, the term "African American" refers to those of us who are part of the African Diaspora that were brought to the colonies that would become the United States of America through the Transatlantic Slave Trade. However, it is possible to be African American and Black, Haitian and Black, Dominican and Black, and a whole host of other nationalities or ethnicities and Black. In this book, "Black" refers to the all-encompassing racial category that people of darker melanated skin may be labeled without the benefit of inquiry. It refers to a skin tone designation more than a place of origin.

The terminology of "Sistah" and "Sister" has distinctions and boundaries. I refer to non-Black women as "Sister" and Black women as "Sistah." The term "Sistah" signifies the communal relationship formed amongst Black women out of our collective history. The relationship is formulated through bonds of laughter as we find reprieve in the village mentality of child-rearing, the sisterhood of the beauty shop, and the sly smile we give each other on the rare occasion we're not the only Black woman in the meeting. The connecting point helps us realize we are not alone in a world that isolates us. We are Sistahs.

The term "Sister" throughout this book is two-folded. First, it refers to any woman that is non-Black. "Sister" also refers to relationships formulated between Black and non-Black women working to build communities of justice and reconciliation.

While the terms are not interchangeable across racial lines, the difference doesn't have to divide us. Before we were Sistahs and Sisters, we were daughters. Before society erected oppression, we were formed from the dust of the Earth, partly created from the rib of Adam, shaped by the hands of God, and given life from the breath of the Divine. In the words of Dr. Martin Luther King, Jr., "our humanity connects us."

Second, while Black and White, Sistah and Sister, are binary phrasings, this is not a binary book. This book will help White women understand Black women but also help all races of women understand what Black women have contributed to American society and the obstacles we are tired of jumping. It will help men of all races understand the unequal systems that women of all races are still contending with. And it will help everyone better understand the inequalities that still need rectifying.

These letters strive to capture the by-and-large experiences of Black women, but this book has some limitations. In reading these letters, remember that Black women are not all the same. While we may hold many of the same ideals and share so much hurtful history and helpful experiences, every letter will not be the experience of every Black woman. These letters are my experiences. Supported by our collective history. And echoed by other women in the community. A different perspective isn't necessarily a dissenting one, just a distinct one.

This book does not address the triple intersectionality of race, gender, and sexuality. I do not wish to minimize the experiences of Black women who are part of the LGBTQIA+ community by pretending that I understand this dynamic. I am not part of the LGBTQIA+ community, and this is not an area of my research focus. My Sistahs in that community may share some of the perspectives in these letters, but they also may have another viewpoint to add. Their view is to be valued and should be heard directly.

My goal for this book is that the information in these letters will be transformational. For my Sistahs, I hope this book represents your experiences accurately and responsibly so you feel seen and heard. For my Sisters, I hope you will see and hear us. See our humanity. Hear our pain. Applaud our victories. And then be willing to keep engaging in conversations and the work that might one day heal the divide.

So, from Sistah to Sister, as well as everyone else who is joining us on this journey, there are some things Black women want you to know.

The Voice of One of the Sistahs,

Paula Dannielle

Dear Sister,
Here's what Black women want you to know . . .

. . . About Showing Up

If each person in this world will simply
take a small piece of this huge thing,
this amazing quilt, and work it regardless of the color of the yarn,
we will have harmony on this planet.

—Cicely Tyson, Actress
Presidential Medal of Freedom recipient
NAACP Image Award recipient

Dear Sister,

Did you know that choreographed dance routines are a normative part of the worship experience in many Black church traditions? While dance ministry leaders have different levels of training, I had over twenty years of training in ballet, modern, and jazz before there was an incident. I was ministering in a church service when I came down out of a leap. I landed on my right foot, and my right ankle rolled over. Now, after two decades of dancing, I was no stranger to rolling ankles, so I finished the dance, walked off the platform, and went to change. But, as I walked out of the sanctuary, even before the adrenaline subsided, I knew this ankle roll was different. Something was wrong. This was more than a twist.

By the time I got in the car, my ankle had started to turn colors. What was once just swollen was now swollen and pur-ple. With urgent care centers closed for the night, my friend insisted on taking me to the emergency room to get checked out. As I waited in the emergency room of Emory Hospital for a few hours, I thought, "This is so dumb! My ankle isn't broken. I can go home, elevate it, ice it, and repeat. In a few days (okay, maybe weeks), I'll be fine." After the doctor final-ly called me to the back and did a quick exam, he ordered an x-ray. When the results came back, I for sure thought that he was exaggerating.

The doctor said three words no dancer ever wants to hear: "It is broken." Even after showing me the x-rays, I insisted it was only sprained. The reality of something so intricate to who I was being broken was frightening. The diagnosis presented more questions than answers. The break presented an uneasiness and instability that I felt ill-equipped to face.

For a few minutes, I argued with the doctor. I wanted a second opinion. What he was seeing on the x-ray was a piece of dust magnified. My ankle wasn't actually broken. Give me a brace. A bag of ice. And I'm good to go! The doctor, growing irritated with my protest, looked me square in the face and said, "Insisting that it is not broken when it is broken will not make it any less broken." Then he put me in a cast and discussed the next several months of treatment and recovery.

My doctor made it abundantly clear that getting the ankle diagnosed was just the first step in achieving healing. It would take more than an acknowledgment of brokenness to bring wholeness. To fully recover from the damage done, I would have to alter the entire way I lived. I'd have to learn how to walk differently, using crutches while in a cast, an ankle boot, and a brace. I'd have to go to physical therapy to strengthen my muscles and learn to walk correctly again. The damage done by one break would change everything for months. My parking would change. It would take me longer to hobble up and down the hills to class. I would need assistance with little things like carrying my coffee. Even going to the grocery store would require help and planning. To recover from the break, I had to alter my life. It changed how I showed up in the world.

My Sister, you are reading these letters, so it is safe to assume that you know something in the relationship from Sistah to Sister is broken. The way we relate to each other isn't always healthy. There is a break in our relationship—a relationship that could do so much good in the world if it were healthy. And like the leap broke my ankle, racism has broken our relationship. The brokenness of racism has been passed down from generation to generation. I know the movies portray that White men are responsible for the racism that Black people have faced in this country, but we—your Sistahs—need you to face the ugly reality that that is simply not the entire truth.

The horrors we have faced as Black women were oftentimes at the hands of the wife of Massa. White women were packing lunch baskets and corralling children to go to the neighborhood lynchings after church that morning. The White lady of the house was denigrating our grandmothers and aunts who were taking care of their children and cleaning their toilets. There were just as many White women yelling at young Black children integrating the schools of the South as there were White men. And in today's business and educational world, Black women contend with having our experience and expertise disregarded by the tears, the giggles, and the intentionally high-pitched voices that come from our White Sisters.

We understand you have dealt with the injustice of chauvinism and sexism. We know that, at times, you may have felt like it was the survival of the fittest. But I want you also to consider that no one truly survives when survival is obtained by the willingness to step on one person experiencing oppression so that you can alleviate the pain of your own. If we were to spend more time walking together, we could heal the damage that chauvinism and racism have done to all of us. Chauvinism and racism are two sides of the same coin because they are both the result of one piece of humanity willing to disparage the image of God in another.

Walking together will require work. It will require being willing to see our pain without feeling the need to play oppression comparison. Without having to say, "White women go through that too." It will require acknowledging differences even when there are similarities.

It will require discomfort and strength and more discomfort. Conversations on race are uncomfortable. It will be hurtful to acknowledge the racial history of this country; one in which, at most, you've benefited from, and at minimum you haven't been held back because of. It will require sitting in conversations that are about the Black experience because that is the one that has been dismissed. The discomfort will lead to conversations where you have to correct family members and close friends when they say something inappropriate. But it will also lead to strength!

As you find the strength to advocate for others who are forgotten, you will find your voice too! You will find the strength to believe that the world can be made better. You will find the fortitude to hold emotional space for others who need the room. The willingness to deal with temporary discomfort will strengthen your resolve for the work that will take all of us.

Walking together will require you to show up! However, like with my ankle, how you personally and collectively show up will have direct implications on how, and if, the break ever heals. It's more than just showing up in spaces and talking about racial reconciliation. The healing will come from how you show up in your everyday life.

Your Sistahs need you to show up by changing your proximity. When you move from distance to proximity and then show up personally and create meaningful relationships with Black women, it can bridge the space that racism created between us. When you show up to listen and learn, you can unlearn the lies racism has told about us and begin to understand the experiences of being a Black woman in this country. When you show up to advocate for our well-being and the undoing of unjust systems, you can help heal how racist practices have harmed our communities. When we show up together, we can create a more unified world.

Sister, let me be honest, just like the treatment for my broken ankle was painful, showing up to heal will be uncomfortable. It may be uncomfortable to ask hard questions and listen to the answers. It may be uncomfortable to diversify your reading and streaming list. It may be uncomfortable to refuse to laugh at the joke about a Black coworker being on "CP time" when she runs late due to normal obstacles that happen to everyone else too. It may be uncomfortable to leverage your privilege to make sure we get the credit and compensation we deserve. It may be uncomfortable to listen to certain hip-hop songs and not say every word or not adopt certain intonations. Regardless of the discomfort, stay in it! Show up! Advocate! Realize that there is a difference between discomfort and pain and, at times, both are necessary to experience change.

When I was going through physical therapy, I hated the exercises that my therapist made me do. First, they hurt! Using those silly elastic bands of varying tensions to lift my ankle one way or the other caused some stretching. But every time I'd complain, my therapist would say, "Does it hurt, or is it uncomfortable?"

Talking about racism is uncomfortable for you, but it is painful for those of us who experience it and have been broken by it. When you show up in a space where racial disparities and systems manifest, we need you to show up ready to deal with your discomfort and address the pain that racism has inflicted on Black women. Be willing and ready to acknowledge and do something to alleviate our pain. The pain caused by your history and the pain that still comes with showing up as a Black woman in this world.

The leap into slavery broke our relationship. Years of racial terror, Jim Crow, and separation broke that relationship. But like my physical therapist told me, and I'm willing to tell you, there are some things you can do to repair it. There are some things you can do to strengthen it. The repair won't be easy. The strengthening won't be comfortable. But if you work with us, we will show you how to show up so we can get it done—together!

With You in Healing,

The Sistahs

About Showing Up

Over one-third of the survey respondents **encouraged women of other races to show up to ight against racism and injustice, however, we want them to show up as themselves** without feeling the need to imitate the cultural nuances of Black women.

Dear Sister,
Here's what Black women want you to know . . .

. . . About My History

Dear Sister,

Reading this letter is not going to be easy. It wasn't easy to write. I found myself holding my breath, taking a breath of relief, only to have it stolen again. But this is the reality of Black history. So, as you read this, you may have your breath stolen too. But I hope you keep reading because before you can understand what your Black Sisters want you to know today, you need to know yesterday's history. You need to understand the systems from the past that created our struggles in the present. So, let's start at the beginning.

More than two hundred and forty-six years of creating false categories of superiority and inferiority based on color and physical characteristics passed before the 13th Amendment ended chattel slavery. Still, it didn't put an end to racism. The formerly enslaved didn't find themselves free, as slave codes restricted their movement, freedoms, and opportunities. When my ancestors secured influence and progress, the Ku Klux Klan was created to reassert White superiority and dominance. Even still, my people pushed for progress.

Black independence and prosperity were established in places like Tulsa, Oklahoma, Durham, North Carolina, and Rosewood, Florida. Black people were building businesses, establishing schools, and receiving medical care from medical professionals of color without the fear of being terrorized. But our retreat didn't last long, and the threat of barbaric killings was always imminent. Since my people wouldn't let go of their ability to build their communities, the government enacted policies to attempt to prevent us from building our dignity.

What racism couldn't kill with lynchings, arson, and bombings, he protected with the establishment of Jim Crow laws. Even when Brown v. the Board of Education was passed in 1954, and the Supreme Court ruled that separate was not equal, White America responded to forced educational integration by establishing more faith-based private schools that would perpetuate segregation under the name of Jesus. I'll never understand how a loving Jesus was used as a viable excuse to perpetuate hate, leverage privilege, and erect more institutions of division. But even while hate was being planted, my elders insisted that this was not the Jesus my generation would inherit. The loving, liberating Christ could not be co-opted by hateful oppression.

The Civil Rights Movement brought people of faith together to eradicate the policies and politics that treated God's people, Black people, less than the image-bearers that we are. My elders proclaimed that people made in the image of God would not sit at different seats because of their pigmentation. My grandparents kneeled in city halls so my generation could participate in government. My mother's generation integrated schools so that my generation would one day create the curriculum that taught everyone that loving others is possible. The faith and fight of that generation resulted in the outlawing of segregated buses in 1956, the passing of the Civil Rights Act of 1964, and the Voting Rights Act of 1965, making protections for equal voting possible. Why only "possible?" Well, because even in 2023, too many cities are still fighting for the enforcement of these provisions and stand under the threat of having the protections afforded to them in 1965 revoked every election cycle.

Even after all of the legislation of the 1950s and 1960s, in 1970, we have racism masked by legal policies that would disproportionately afflict Black communities with the growth of the Prison Industrial Complex. Nope! Not a mistake. It's "afflict" and not "affect." The Prison Industrial Complex didn't just "affect" our communities. It evoked suffering, pain, and terror on countless communities with policies and practices that were so disproportionately unjust, many of them have been stopped, overturned, or are being investigated today. And I wish this was the end of my list. But Black people have also contended with redlining, gentrification, the school-to-prison pipeline, and predatory lending practices just to name a few.

Do you feel a twinge of oratory whiplash reading what I just described? If you do, I get it, because I feel the back-and-forth, heartbreaking tug while writing it. I've felt the exhale of hope only to have to inhale in despair at another racist-induced setback. Our generations didn't get a chance to recover while experiencing it, so forgive me, but I have difficulty giving unrealistic recovery time while writing it. Racism, unlike energy, was created, and while it has yet to be so, it can be destroyed. Unfortunately, as of now, it has only changed form as we've moved from one generation to another. Where America was founded on legal racism, the last few decades have seen the enactment of policies and practices that have expanded social racism.

Just as White people held the majority of political and legal power, they held power to set the standards for what would be labeled as "appropriate" in culture. That means White culture became the standard for correctness, and White was declared right! Not only is that White standard too often seen as neutral, but anything different is deemed inferior. White people had straight hair, so the standard was straight. White people defined the words in the dictionary and the grammar in schools, so "is not" was normal, while "'ain't' ain't a word." White people had the power to establish normalcy, and racism relegated everything and everyone else as abnormal portraying cultural differences as cultural inferiority.

I became aware of society's view of my race and culture as inferior at a young age. The first Disney princess I remember was Cinderella. Then there was Snow White. I remember Belle and Ariel (the first one). I loved them all! Many of the songs I knew. And for years, I wondered if people were really sure that there were no mermaids under the sea. Guess what all of these princesses had in common? None of them looked like me! Wasn't my skin pretty enough to be on the body of a Disney princess? Wouldn't the curls on my head fit under a princess crown? Could I marry a prince or could a knight in shining armor rescue me? Subliminally the message was clear, Black girls couldn't be princesses. Black girls couldn't be pretty. And no one was interested in saving us.

It wasn't until 1997 that I'd see that little Black girls can be portrayed as princesses. Little Black girls can have their fairy-tales come true. We can have the "impossible" show up for us, too. Brandy said so! As a sophomore in high school, I sat in my living room with my sister and mother, when Brandy told us it's possible for a plain country bumpkin and a prince to join in marriage. And Whitney Houston became our fairy godmother and told a generation of Black girls that impossible things were happening every day! Roger and Hammerstein, in their 1997 version of *Cinderella*, changed a cultural narrative that never should've existed in the first place.

This was an important moment in history, but make-believe is still make-believe. Black girls of my generation got to become princesses in Cinderella. Black girls of this current generation will see their skin tone reflected in a new Ariel. And while these are culturally important, value-affirming moments, where are Black girls seeing themselves in reality? Are they seeing themselves in standards of beauty on social media? Are they seeing their intellect and ability to lead highlighted in the books in their classrooms? Are we taking children on field trips that show the contributions of the people of color in this country? America is not a fairytale so we have to show up for children of color in real life.

And before you say, "I don't have or know any children of color," the society you create for children of color will affect society for everybody. So, how do you create a better society? Every society has rules and norms, but what if those rules and norms came down to valuing others as you want others to value you? We show value for others when we watch shows and movies with main characters that don't look like us. We learn and value other cultural experiences when we read books that are written by authors who are different from us. And we force the media to respond to our demand for diversity.

In America, we change society by how we vote. When we go to the polls, we vote for interests that protect the rights of the marginalized, the left out, and those who have been historically oppressed. We change society by not pledging an allegiance to a political party, but to an ideal that government is not just for people that agree with me, but should protect the rights of life and liberty for people who may not agree with me. We vote like we take the Fourteenth Amendment seriously that "no state shall make or enforce any law which shall abridge the privileges or immunities of citizens of the United States." We vote like history matters and repentance is important for change.

When we meet with city and school officials, we create a different society, by being willing to tell the truth about the society we have been. We refuse to silence the authors who are writing about the truth of injustice by which this country was founded. We raise our children in spaces where their ideas may not be the only ideas in the room, so that they can learn to respect the ideas that are different. We intentionally put them in situations where they are uncomfortable so that when they become adults, they don't criminalize individuals that are unfamiliar. We change society by creating a world where diversity is treasured as a byproduct of reconciliation with our neighbor.

Sisters. Creating a better tomorrow starts with telling the truth about yesterday. Not on Disney. But in reality. We have inherited a mess. True! Racism was here before we were born. True! And this world doesn't have to be the world we give the next generation. Most true! What has been true of the past does not have to stop the truth of what can be in the future. My hope is these letters will help you see the lies that need to be dismantled and the injustices that must be corrected so that we can first change our relationships, and through a better understanding, we can change the world by healing the divide from Sistah to Sister.

Working for Tomorrow,

The Sistahs

About Our History

Comments about segregation, racism, and slavery said as a joke are hurtful.

Acknowledge racism still exists. White privilege is a thing, and Black women do not get the same opportunities as White women.

We are not a historical resource. Get to know the Black women you meet individually, be a good listener, ask about allyship, and read up on historical events that have impacted Black women disproportionately.

We have rich histories. Our history starts well before slavery.

Even at varying levels, there is a system designed to oppress us both. We are better together.

If you engage in a conversation surrounding social justice, be open to having your perspective challenged and presented within a context that may be unfamiliar to you.

Not speaking up is just like agreeing or siding with any acts of racism that you witness or hear about.

Don't say the N-word whether singing, rapping, or trying to be "endearing."

Know and understand the history of Black people in this country.

Racism is still very much alive.

Black women will survive no matter what you try to do to ensure that doesn't happen.

It is impossible to change what is if one refuses to look at what was. Black women overwhelmingly want others to acknowledge the pain that we've suffered and the contributions we've made for **the benefit of all of society.**

Dear Sister,
Here's what Black women want you to know . . .

. . . About My Sistahs

When you're a black woman,
you seldom get to do what you just want to do;
you always do what you have to do.

—Dorothy Height
Civil Rights Leader
President of National Council of Negro Women

Dear Sister,

I know the media would have us think that all Black women are the same, but that couldn't be further from the truth. While race is a huge contributing factor to how many of us view the world, it is not the only factor. One's culture is created from more than just their skin color. And while experience creates culture, history influences the collective that is "the Sistahs."

I grew up in a mostly White area in the suburbs of Phoenix. While everybody I went to church with was Black, and my friends I took dance lessons with on Saturdays were Black, my classmates and teachers were White. This meant I had a hard time seeing myself in the world around me five out of seven days a week. I remember the first time my skin got a little dry at school—the result of the scorching heat and the dry "Valley of the Sun" climate. A classmate of mine looked down at my legs and told me I was turning white because she had never seen what "ash" does to melanated skin. I remember going to a friend's house and not being able to get in the pool. Back then, and still to some degree, chlorine had some damaging effects on my relaxer-treated hair. I remember going to the house of a White friend and realizing some kids do not "put a handle" on an adult's name. Everyone was on a first-name basis. I'm 42 years old, and I still hesitate to not add the "Mr." or "Ms." on the name of one of my elders. From a young age, I knew there were differences between White and Black people. Those differences occur between Black women too.

Race influences how we experience the world and how we show up in it. Because of the history of the United States, race has a significant influence on culture. For hundreds of years, people were put in communities by this one factor. For Black Americans, including those of African descent but not exclusively so, Black culture is something we created because our African cultures were stripped away when the yolks of chattel slavery were placed on us. So, while there are norms and values in Black culture, these norms and values vary. The culture, or outlook, of Black Americans is influenced by more than race. In other words, our culture is not monolithic.

Culture is how we experience the world around us. It influences how we navigate current events and situations. Our culture influences how we interpret the actions, behaviors, and mannerisms of others as well. Culture is more than a demographic category. Culture is an outlook, a way of being, influenced by various demographics, including race.

Looking at Black people in Phoenix, St. Louis, Los Angeles, and Atlanta, you will encounter very different cultures. The jargon you hear will be different. The food may be different or at least cooked differently. And family dynamics may differ. The music, dances, clothing, and interpretation of current events will all be different. There will probably be a baseline of familiarity, but the baseline will be affected by geography, economics, gender, and various social experiences and religious beliefs.

I've experienced these cultural nuances within my own family. My children were born in Arizona but primarily raised in the South. Their way of being is heavily influenced by their formative years spent in Decatur, Georgia and Charlotte, North Carolina. They were taught to address adults with a "handle" (Mr., Ms., Pastor, Doctor), just like their cousins in Phoenix. But you may also hear them answer with a "Sir" or "Ma'am" when you call their name or ask them a question. They tend to hold their vowels a little longer than their cousins, as their southern drawl is apparent to the family in the West. At a recent family gathering, when they walked into the room, their overall energy was different. And if I'm honest, I noticed it was a little different too. No better. No worse. Just different. It wasn't Arizona.

Cooking is different in the South than in the West. Just ask my mom. Recently on a visit from Arizona, she discovered I cooked differently in North Carolina when she found no fatback in my collard greens, but tasted smoked turkey, onion, and tri-colored bell pepper. She was also surprised by the addition of ground beef to my BBQ baked beans—a recipe she now loves but a trick I learned from my folks-that-became-family while I lived in Decatur. And while some of my recipes have a touch of southern flavor, I will never understand shrimp and grits. That southern delicacy didn't pass my cultural palette. To be fair, while my mom doesn't understand all of my cooking methods now, I don't understand some of the culinary combinations from my people in the Midwest. Catfish and spaghetti? Yes, St. Louis and Chicago, I'm looking at you! What? Two main dishes at one time? Like why?

While these differences are geographical, even if you are comparing Black women who live in the same neighborhood, cook the same foods, and use the same expressions, there will be differences because humans have differences. That may seem like an obvious statement, but one we wish more people remembered. When it's assumed all Black women can dance, all of us sing, we all cook, and one of us can speak for all of us on cultural, social, and political issues, you aren't giving the range of our differences the dignity they deserve.

While our everyday preferences may be different, unfortunately, there are traumas, past and present, that give us a collective perspective. There are realities that Black women experience as a community of people that influences the way that we maneuver and interpret the world.

The reality is that past and present traumas tell us that too much of the world believes that Black women don't feel. Like physically, history portrays the story that Black women don't feel pain! This idea has been passed down from generation to generation. When we were used as gynecological testers being forced to undergo feminine procedures without anesthesia, we felt that. When slave masters raped us, our bodies and spirits felt that. Even today, the lack of believing our pain too often leads to our deaths. Black women are still three times more likely to die in childbirth than White women, oftentimes because of a medical professional's disbelief in Black women's pain.[2]

It's not that we don't feel; it is that too much of America continues to believe that we don't. So, our collective response has often been one of distrust and defense against a system that has repeatedly hurt us.

Like our physical pain, our emotional pain is often dismissed by others and has to be put on the shelf and ignored within ourselves. Again, that doesn't mean we don't have emotional pain. It just means that society has made it all-but-impossible for us to tend to it. We are forced to hold our wounds together with the façade of strength that looks like wholeness. Like stitches holding together a gaping wound, the stitches are strong, but the wound is still there. The stitches keep it from bleeding all over others. The stitches protect it from infection. But the presence of strong stitches doesn't mean the absence of a sensitive wound.

Strong is for survival. We don't have the privilege to be weak. Black women have depression too. We suffer from chronic anxiety at higher rates than our White counterparts.[3] But the mental health field is just starting to understand and acknowledge that our symptoms look different. The prevalence of uterine fibroids, numbness, obesity, and constant headaches are outward signs of the, too many times, undiagnosed emotional pain of depression and anxiety.[4] Our wounds are crying out for some place that is safe enough for us to experience healing.

I thought migraine headaches were something that I would suffer with for the rest of my life. I dealt with it from the time I was a child. I changed my diet. I got plenty of exercise. Sleep was not a problem. No matter what I did, they were never ending, always reoccurring.

I remember having the first one in third grade, screaming and rolling around my bed in pain, and no one could figure out what was wrong with me. I dealt with the crippling headaches through adolescence and all of adulthood.

Even through therapy, it was never brought up. Why? My therapist didn't know to ask if I had them, and I didn't know to tell her that I did. Who's ever heard of migraines as a sign of anxiety? Plus, anxiety?!?! Are Black women even allowed to be scared? Are we allowed to be nervous? And you want to take it to anxiety? Chil' please!

But that's exactly what it was! I didn't know until my work climate drastically changed. I was finally making a livable wage. I left a dysfunctional marriage. I was working reasonable hours. And my supervisor was stellar. I was sitting at home one evening, and realized, "Wait, the headaches stopped!" The wounds that were manifesting through migraines were healed the longer I was in a secure home and work environment.

Our emotional strength has been a requirement for survival, not an aspiration for gloating. During slavery, when our babies were snatched away and sold, there was no room for tears. While White women were outlawed from working, it was illegal in some states for us to stay at home and raise our children. While our children are diagnosed with learning differences at disproportionate rates, and then discouraged from pursuing their educational goals and achievements, we have to fight with administrators and school counselors. When we speak with our supervisors about microaggressions, we are accused of being too sensitive. So, we push it down and choose between emotional vulnerability or physical survival.

Not only is our physical and emotional pain ignored and not believed, our bodies are hypersexualized. We are too frequently minimized to the size of our breasts and the span of our hips. While our genetics, stress, and diet affect our body shape, our body shape does not dictate our mental capacity. This hypersexualization overshadows the fact that we are doctors, lawyers, engineers, and scientists. We are politicians and teachers, therapists and pastors, and we continue to excel in the halls of academia, on the floor of Congress, and in the boardrooms of corporate America. So, we push ourselves into exhaustion to prove that we are more than our bodies.

We show up to toxic work environments while having outward signs of inward trauma because not showing up is not a choice. And still, how many times have you complimented a Black woman on her hair, attire, or body shape more than her contributions to the project, the reorganization of the company, or the growth of an organization? How many Black women have been uplifted for their non-physiological contributions to society? Hypersexualization casts a shadow over too many of our other contributions.

Black women have a lot of individual distinctions, but we all feel, we all get tired, and we all want to be valued. There is beauty between us that is missed when you attempt to erase our differences. Yet the history our people have endured and the society we still navigate, bind us together as a collective with similar, not identical, outlooks. In other words, to know one Black woman is to know ONE Black woman. Even though many aspects of our stories are the same, we are beautifully different.

We need you, Sisters, to see the differences while acknowledging the reality of the injustices we face that make us a collective. It is a collective with inherited membership that people only seem to want access to when it puts them on the popular side of culture. Do you want to understand the collective better? This is a great place to start. Continue to read our stories. Dive into our history. Hold your hands and hearts open to receive what we're telling you. But even better than understanding us as a collective, is getting to know us individually. As people! Whole humans! Refusing to minimize us to stereotypical caricatures. And as you open yourself to relationships with us, we will continue to be open to relationships with you so that we can value each other.

Valuing Our Individuality and Commonality,

The Sistahs

About Our Sistahs

Not all Black women think alike. My viewpoint may often be influenced by the amount of prejudice or trauma I've experienced.

Most of us are secure in our skin and no longer feel we have to change our hair texture or how we speak.

Not a single day goes by when I'm not forced to think about being a Black woman in America. I do not realistically have the option of "colorblindness."

We are approachable. Your way of approaching us is everything. If done without respect or making your intentions known, then the door to conversation may close rather quickly.

My dialect is not a joke. My culture is not a personality trait.

We are the most neglected, disrespected, underprotected group of people, and the first to protect you, support you, and pray for you.

We are softer, yet carrying more, than people often realize. We deserve to be handled with care, as we are breakable, like anyone else.

The "strength" of Black women is a result of necessity, as much as it is a tool for survival and success.

Black women are not monolithic. We have shared experiences, places of origin, and similar customs. Yet, across the African diaspora (The United States of America, the Caribbean, Africa, Europe, and wherever else people of African descent are located), our ethnicity, language, and culture are quite different.

46% of Black women included answers pertaining to others seeing them as people. Black women want others to see our vulnerability along with our strength. Our unified struggle alongside our diverse outlooks. **It's time America realized our complexities.**

Dear Sister,

Here's what Black women want you to know . . .

. . . About My Family

If we have the courage and tenacity of our forebears,
who stood firmly like a rock against the lash of slavery,
we shall find a way to do for our day what they did for theirs.

—Mary McLeod Bethune
Educator, Activist, Founder
of Bethune-Cookman University

Dear Sister,

We need to talk about the misconception that Black families can't take care of themselves, that Black men are absent or dead-beat fathers, and Black single mothers are welfare queens. Yeah, we're going there. But before we do, let's visit the backdrop of the African American family. Let's start at New Year's Eve.

What comes to mind when you think of New Year's Eve? Is it sparkly dresses or sparkling drinks? Is it watching the ball drop in Times Square? Maybe your family gathers with snacks and favorite foods to watch a movie. Or maybe it's going to sleep early because you can't hang.

On New Year's Eve, my family cooks black-eyed peas and collard greens. We eat together. And get a nap in because later that evening, we will gather at church. We will sing and celebrate what God has done in the last 365 days. There will be some type of Gospel-centered, hope-filled message presented through music, dance, drama, preaching, and other artistic declaration. We will pray as the clock strikes midnight and then audibly praise God for the fact that we made it into a new year. The elders may be cooking so that we can have breakfast before departing to our homes. It's Watch Night Service!

Why "Watch Night?" Well, because that is what my ancestors were doing on December 31, 1862. Word had traveled, and thanks to one of the provisions in the Emancipation Proclamation, slaves in many, although not all, of the rebelling states of the Confederacy were watching for the night to pass because, on the next day, they would be legally free. Before that, my ancestral families had nothing to celebrate. Before this date, December 31 was a sobering day of realization that this might be the last day we, our families, would be together.

Before there were Watch Night services, there were over 200 years of what is known as "Heartbreak Day." January 1 was one of the most dreaded days in the Antebellum South for my enslaved ancestors because it was the busiest day for the trading, renting, and selling of our family members.

Whether the sale of my ancestors happened on the auction block with a clean bill of sale or at a trade on the side of the road as part of some debt-resolving deal, White families were getting rich or alleviating themselves of debt—while mine were being used for currency and property accrual. Each new year for our families started with children being ripped away from their parents and husbands away from their wives. Even at the Emancipation Proclamation, this would not be the end of ripping Black families apart.

While the end of the Civil War would eventually end chattel slavery, the pattern of ripping the Black Family apart would continue—through lynchings, the Jim Crow era, the War on Poverty, the so-called War on Drugs, and other policies and practices that continued for generations. Separation. Celebration. Separation. Celebration. Again, and again. Most Black people have experienced the lingering impacts of this reality.

I was born in Phoenix, Arizona in 1981 to an affluent family of great reputation. My grandfather was the only Black dentist in Arizona for many years. Mentorship was a priority for him, so he intentionally trained other Black dentists who followed in his footsteps, so that our community had a network of Black dentists to choose from. Grandpa had a long tenure serving as the Chair of the Trustee Ministry at First Institutional Baptist Church, the largest Black church in Phoenix at the time. "Doc," as the community would respectfully reference him, regularly served as an advisor to community leaders. Equally as influential, my grandmother, known in the community as "Momma C," was a short woman with a generously loving reputation. She led the youth ministry for many years and managed the church's kitchen and food pantry, both of which are prominent positions within the African American church. If you visit the church today, you will see her name on a plaque outside the kitchen door in honor of her service.

As a young girl, Sunday mornings with my grandparents were my favorite. We sat in the fifth pew back from the front to the left of the pulpit. From that seat, I gave my life to Jesus at five years old, and the pastor, Rev. Dr. Warren H. Stewart, Sr., baptized me. After the 7:30 a.m. worship service, we had donuts from Winchell's Donut Shop and orange juice before Sunday school. I spent many afternoons and Saturdays in the church basement, watching my grandmother serve the congregation while organizing food boxes for hungry neighbors. Much of who I am today is because of my grandparents and my early years at 1411 East Jefferson Street. My grandparents were married for 52 years before my grandmother passed away on December 12, 1996.

My grandparents had four biological children who made their own marks in the world. My uncle is an honored soldier who served as a medic in the Vietnam War. My aunts integrated the Phoenix Suns cheerleading team. This achievement was significant when Black was not deemed beautiful as Sistahs didn't meet the standard of beauty with long blonde hair and blue eyes. Their Black Girl Magic extended as they both went on to have careers in the legal and cosmetology fields. The youngest child of my grandparents, my mother, was in the financial industry until the economic downturn of 1990. Then, she returned to college, earning a master's in Educational Leadership and working in our educational system for the next 28 years. Even as I write this book, at 69 years old, she's teaching today.

And these were just my grandparents' biological children. I have countless surrogate aunts, uncles, and cousins that my grandparents put through college, led to follow Jesus, mentored through marriage, and helped develop purposeful lives. Their offspring, biological and non, lead in prominent churches, head up Historically Black Colleges and Universities, serve on corporate boards, work in law enforcement, and governmental spaces. We believe in family and the power of community!

While my family is no stranger to prestige and prominence, we've also felt the impact of America's injustice on Black people as my family was torn apart at various points. In 1978, my mother married a preacher from Los Angeles, California. Due to the lack of care offered to Black Vietnam War vets, his exposure to Agent Orange went undiagnosed for many years. As a result, their marriage would become one of many casualties my family would face over the next two generations.

While both Black and White men returned home with PTSD, mental illnesses, and struggles from chemical dependency, there were disparities in how resources and support were distributed. As the untreated effects from the war and Agent Orange poisoning drew my father further and further away from reality and responsibility, he would eventually disappear from my life. My mother was left to raise three children in a loving community, but now also a single mother. His absence could've meant a detrimental impact on my story, but the Black community has a long tradition of fighting for family.

Family is a term that is wide and inclusive. Family does not stop at blood relatives. We can be family and share no DNA. Being family has just as much to do with who you were born to as much as it has to do with who is helping to raise you, care for you, has been given permission to speak into your life, and correct you. We have aunts not related to our parents and cousins not related to their siblings. Family is an all-inclusive word that refers to people who have been given an unwavering license and expectation to care. Our history makes this usage of the word helpful and necessary.

Because of our communal senses, while my father may not have been in the home, my siblings and I were not without positive male influences. My Uncle Andy was an 18-wheel truck driver who would come off the road long enough to take us to Dairy Queen. My Uncle Alton kept my mother amusingly agitated by teaching us things every mother would despise, but every uncle would think is hilarious. And my Uncle Jim, a White man adopted into the village, would fix what was needed and keep maintenance bills low. All three uncles. Not one of them blood relatives. And while I already mentioned to you the role my grandfather and biological uncle, Greg, played in the community, they were also active in my life and the lives of my siblings.

I know the stories you have been told perpetuate a narrative that the Black family is a chaotic institution barely caring for itself. But that could not be farther from the truth. The truth is we've always cared for our own, even as White America has done all it can to create systems of great chaos. From the emasculation of Black men by lynching their naked bodies from trees to the imprisonment of Black fathers with sentences disproportionately longer than their White counterparts, the attempts have been immeasurable and the results crippling.

As America continues to implement policies that disproportionately emasculate and remove Black men from their homes, Black women are left to fill in the gaps and provide two-parent roles by one person. As more and more Black women became single mothers due to these disparaging policies, they were portrayed as welfare queens taking money from hard-working Americans—even though the original woman, Linda Taylor, was an outlier who Ronald Reagan leveraged for political expediency in one of his 1976 presidential candidacy speeches. And she was biracial, often using wigs and clothes to change and hide her racial identity.

Black fathers and Black mothers are present. They are working hard to provide and protect. Even in the 21st century, too much of the public narrative tells of a disengaged Black father and the singleness of the Black mother, while it has been statistically proven that Black fathers are more involved in the lives of their children than any other racial or ethnic group.[5] Stereotypes and historical mythology still threaten to upend our family dynamics as we have to force our children to think and act like adults before it's time.

Our children have to be taught that society often sees them as a threat before their brains have been developed to handle the emotional stress that comes with that reality. Many of you reading my letter are old enough to remember the Central Park Five—now the Exonerated Central Park Five—who were young boys dubbed teenage thugs before the trial about the heinous assault of a White woman even began. Tamir and his family know the reality that playing on the playground poses the danger that your toy gun will be mistaken as a real one. Shakarra, a then 16-year-old girl in South Carolina, found out she could be manhandled out of her school desk, pinned to the floor, thrown across the room, and handcuffed over a cell phone. And who has ever experienced a six-year-old having a temper tantrum? Well, in Florida, little Kaia found out that she doesn't get to have a six-year-old meltdown when she was arrested, put in handcuffs, carried out of school by two police officers, and thrown into the back of a police car.

For our community, the first days of school come with fears of a schoolyard scuffle becoming a prison sentence. Shopping for clothes comes with lessons to keep our hoodies down. It's hard to be a child when your skin tone causes you to be seen as a threat. It's hard to have childhood innocence when you are not afforded the privilege of being presumed innocent. It's impossible to be protected in a society that dubs your skin tone a criminality trait.

All of this trauma erects hurdles to children becoming healthy adults as they are forced to skip the natural maturation process that children of other races are privileged to matriculate through. It disrupts familial patterns and causes generational dysfunction. Subliminal messages and explicit bias become self-fulfilling prophecies that we spend a lifetime fighting against.

With the numerous attempts to build strong families that I've listed here, and the many more that have gone unsaid, Sisters, I have a question. How many times can you hit something before it breaks? This is not a riddle. It is the reality of the Black family and a question that America has been trying to solve by swinging its proverbial hammer at it for more than 400 years.

With all the Black family has suffered, and statistically, they continue to thrive, why does America continue to paint her with a brush of dysfunction? Could it be that as Black and White people continue to navigate life from different vantage points, the gap between reality and myth is being widened?

If that is the problem, then proximity is only part of the solution. Sure, it helps to have neighbors of color and make sure your children experience life outside of a bubble of racial homogeneity. But the other part of the solution comes with recognizing how our stories are even told. In reality, Black children need the same maturational space afforded to White children. They need to be able to have hard days at school without being forced into the school-to-prison pipeline. A child needs to be able to play with a toy gun without a mother having to arrange his funeral. A Black mother needs to be able to leave a domestically violent relationship without being painted as irresponsible herself. And Black fathers need to be seen as individuals who do care for their children and wives in real life and on cinematic screens. Sister, we need you to change more than your proximity. We want you to adjust your lens and change your perspective.

You have a part to play in dismantling the myth that Black fathers are derelict, Black mothers are loose and lazy, and Black children are a threat to society. You know White men that suffer from mental illness or chemical dependency. Black men deserve the same treatment and resources you'd give to your husband, brother, or son. You know White women who have fallen victim to circumstance and are doing all they can to hold it together. She needs friendship more than pity and the benefit of the doubt more than a judgment based on erroneous stereotypes. You know White children who have hard days at school, and they get sent home with a note saying, "Let's try it again tomorrow." None of these situations point to a lack of love. You still love your family members and assume the best of your community members, even at their worst. Can you do the same for ours?

Take the reading of my letter as an opportunity to decide not only to check your own bias, but to speak out when you hear it from others. It's not enough to dispel a lie. It's also important to speak the truth. The truth is the Black family has been assaulted. The wounds that we are fighting to heal were caused by a history we didn't write or construct. These wounds are the result of hundreds of years of blows. Yet we have survived. One fight after another, we continue to thrive. Make no bones about it, we will continue to get in the ring and fight for what is ours. Love. Family. Legacy. And the dispelling of the myth that we work for anything less. No matter how hard injustice punches against it. Because we are…

Fighting For Our Families,

The Sistahs

About Our Family

If marrying a Black man and having his children, learn to do their hair or regularly have someone maintain it.

Don't tell us that "mixed babies" are the most beautiful or that this is the reason you want to have a child by a Black man. It's offensive.

Dating Black men and having Black babies doesn't absolve you from doing work to be a better person. Anti-racist work is a lifelong commitment.

Some Black women are not bothered by some Black men who choose White women.

Our men are not your fetish.

We don't…and can't…raise our children the same. While some of our mothering challenges are the same, there are many that are extremely different.

Having Black children and not educating them on the Black experience is a form of abuse.

We often make decisions based on the communal good and progression, often at the expense of ourselves.

How we parent may be different. Respect is more important than being liked or being my child's friend.

Our experiences with patriarchy are different.

It's okay to have a different opinion than your family members and ancestral tradition.

Racism has made it challenging for Black women to get married and be loved by men of all races, **but we are particularly concerned about being accepted by our own.** Rejection by a community that you've been responsible for cultivating is doubly hurtful.

Dear Sister,
Here's what Black women want you to know . . .

. . . About My Hair

In a dream, a big black man appeared to me
and told me what to mix up for my hair.
I made up my mind I would begin to sell it.

—Madam C.J. Walker
Hair Culturist
First Female Self-Made Millionaire

Dear Sister,

Our hair doesn't happen by accident. I'm not just referring to the growth of it, but oftentimes the way we wear it. Black women spend an average of $54.14 per month on their hair and contribute to an industry with an estimated value of $2.5 billion, projected to reach over $6.9 billion by 2026. There is a plethora of reasons for this but with this kind of investment, and even for my Sistahs who fall outside of these numbers, one thing is abundantly clear: please, do not touch our hair!

"Don't scratch!" When I think back on those Saturdays, this is the statement I remember most. When I was three years old, my mom would spend ten hours on Saturday preparing my and my sister's hair for church on Sunday and for school the rest of the week. Preparation didn't happen in the shower. It started on the cabinet of my grandmother's kitchen sink. Shampoo. Lather. Rinse. Shampoo. Lather. Rinse. Shampoo. Lather Rinse. THREE TIMES! Yes, you read that correctly! THREE TIMES! Because that is what it took to get the thick, tightened curls that hung down my back, all the way to my backside, clean. Hop down off the sink. Towel dry. Put on hair conditioner. Comb through in small sections and braid it down. Processing cap on. And wait! While I waited, my mom started the same process with my younger sister's hair. After repeating the shampoo routine with my sister's hair, I hopped back onto the cabinet to rinse out the conditioner. One pre-braided section at a time. Back down off the kitchen sink. Re-braid the hair into eight sections this time. Blow dry with the wide-tooth comb. Then the small tooth comb. Loosely braid back up. Section one—done! And repeat. Seven. More. Times.

Wait! Don't get tired! We're only halfway done. The process continued at the kitchen stove, where a metal comb was placed on a heated eye effectively making it a "hot comb." My mom would take a few strands of hair, apply Blue Magic hair grease, and slowly run the heated metal comb through it, finalizing the straightening process. After I got a few minutes to run around the house, swinging the hair that ran down my back from side to side, it was time to style it. Correct! We hadn't styled it yet. Rubber bands. Barrettes. Hairballs. And twisted or braided-up pigtails that would last another few weeks. This routine lasted until my mother had enough. I was five years old when she reached her wits-end with my hair. She was done spending ten hours on a Saturday fighting with her two girls. Off to the beauty shop we went like so many other little Black girls our age.

My mother will tell you that we were kicked out of three salons before she found someone that would put a relaxer on my hair. I was too young. Too tender-headed. And had too much hair. She searched endlessly in Phoenix for a stylist that would take the creamy lye chemical and place it on my roots and comb it through my hair every six weeks for $70 in 1986 to straighten my curls and make it easier to manage. But for it to work and not waste time and money, my scalp couldn't be touched. My mom was constantly watching for the slightest movement of my arm. "NO SCRATCHING!"

In relaxer preparation, there were two cardinal rules a few days before the relaxing process started. No tension on the scalp. No itching of the scalp whatsoever! If you forgot and your hand subconsciously moved to scratch your head, the burn of the relaxer the next day would let you know. Now instead of an itchy scalp, you would have a burned and scabby one.

That's painful, but nothing compared to if you also had to remove the chemical early. If you did, you could even have partially processed hair affecting your texture and, at times, hair loss. A two-second scratch could turn into weeks of messed up hair before you even had the possibility of starting the process over again. And those few weeks feel like a lifetime to a self-conscious kid or teenager.

So, you might ask, "Why would anybody put themselves or their child through this ordeal?" This is what you do when you are a Black girl living in a society with White beauty standards. According to society, beautiful hair means straight hair. That was confirmed by every Barbie doll with dark skin and straight hair, every Disney princess with long wavy, not even curly strands, and every ballet recital that required a perfect bun (which is almost impossible with tight curls). Not conforming to these standards, at best, resulted in ridicule and, at worst, criminalization.

This standard was not just enforced for little girls. Black professional women straightened our curls to increase our chances for acceptance and promotion because our natural hair has long been considered unprofessional. We let go of our afros and were reluctant to wear braids. The application of the relaxer was not just our choice of hairstyle. It was an adaptation for survival.

This survival tactic was so prominent that in 2019, California passed the CROWN Act (Creating a Respectful and Open World for Natural Hair) to lessen the disparity in how Black people are treated because of our hair. Twenty-two other states have passed varying versions of this law since then. One of the purposes of legislation in this country is to protect people's rights to life, liberty, and the pursuit of happiness. The demands that have been placed on Black women regarding their hair has stolen all three of those.

Remember the relaxers that I spoke about enduring for over 30 years of my life? Well, now we are learning that those chemicals that we put on our hair in order to meet the "presentable" standard in educational and professional settings actually lead to cancer. That's right! Many Black women have been forced to make the choice between taking in carcinogens or losing a job. It was, "Either put this chemical on your hair, or we will take the liberty you have to pursue this job for your livelihood and your pursuit of happiness."

Were you aware that Black girls, without the protective legislation of versions of the CROWN Act, were being suspended from school? You read that right. Eleven-year-old Faith Fennidy was suspended from Christ the King Elementary School in Terrytown, Louisiana for wearing a braiding style to protect her hair after the school added a prohibition to braids in their rulebook over the summer. She missed valuable time of instruction and was shamed in front of her classmates. Christ the King used Faith's cultural and necessary hairstyle to deprive her of her right to an education. Louisiana responded to this and other cases by finally passing CROWN Act legislation in 2022.

We continue to have to fight for the right to show up. We are in court battles, human resources meetings, and discussions with school administrators to convince people that our curls, locs, and braids are not an affront to anybody; but America's obsession with trying to make Black people look like everyone else is an assault against who God created us to be. Straight hair. Curly hair. Wavy hair. Long hair. Short hair. Braids or extensions. It is mine! And I should be able to show up with me in any room. Our hair is personal.

The personal nature of our hair, along with all we have to go through to protect it, thickens our boundary against you touching it. Whether we've invested in maintaining our curls, decided to straighten our coils, or braided or twisted it up, we've made an investment in our person and then you cross the boundary and touch her. "Boundary" may seem like an interesting word choice, but it is intentional. A boundary is a line that marks a limit. A place that should not be crossed. Since we teach kids this social norm at a very young age, to keep their hands to themselves and to not touch people without permission, I must admit, I'm a little confused. Why are Black women forced to accept this level of violation when we wear hairstyles appropriate for our hair texture and reflective of our culture? Why are we not afforded this norm and instead treated like animals in a zoo?

If you don't believe me, consider this story from my colleague that wears locs. She was in a store when a White individual walked up to her and asked to "pet" her hair. Pet! Like, they actually used the word "PET!" Pet is what you do to animals! Not people! And Black people are PEOPLE! Think of the motion your hands take when you rub your fingers through an individual's hair. It is similar, if not precisely what we do to cats, dogs, or sheep at the petting zoo. I know of another lady who had somebody grab her braids and pull them like horse reins. Black women should not be treated as if we belong in exhibits, probed and petted as if we are exotic. We're allowed to have boundaries. We are not the property of your curiosity.

Here's what's true: curiosity becomes exploitation when someone assumes familiarity. *Healthy* curiosity takes a posture of not knowing while refraining from assuming familiarity, admiring from a physical distance without violating personal space or asking researchable questions. My friend, Jen, put it like this: "If you see someone with beautiful teeth, you might say your teeth are gorgeous. You would never reach into their mouth and try to feel out why their teeth look the way they do. You would never say, 'Your teeth are beautiful. Are they real?'" You might be chuckling, but seriously, no one would ever think of crossing that boundary. The same principle applies.

Now you might be thinking, but what if I ask them and they say yes? Let me pose a question to your question. Have you ever asked someone to do something or have something and expected them to say no? Of course not; no one asks a question expecting not to get what they are asking for! And using the example above, would you ask someone to touch their beautiful teeth? Of course not! The question itself assumes that you should and will be told yes. And since we're trying to give you some secrets to building sisterhood, here's one I really want you to remember: Asking to touch my hair puts me in the precarious position of having to say no. Instead, can you just refrain from even asking?

In addition, let me take a second to point out the historical power dynamic at play during these interactions. Our country just recently acknowledged that Black women have legal agency over our own bodies. Let us keep it.

Asking to touch our hair assumes that you are owed our "yes." The question implies that you have the right to have your curiosity resolved by touching my person. It implies that you have the right to know. It says, "I have the right to have my curiosity answered. I deserve to know. I deserve to know how your locs feel. I deserve to know how your braids are parted in squares. I deserve to know if your curls feel how they look. I deserve…". I need you to embrace that you lose your right to know when it violates my right to be. Be in my space. Be in my skin. Be within my boundary.

Sisters, your curiosity doesn't entitle you to the level of familiarity that is needed before you are given the privilege, not the right, to know. Familiarity is earned in genuine relationships, and trust is built over time.

I have some White friends who can ask about the intricacies of my hairstyle, and they have been my friends for years. They are with me in celebrations and in hard times. When I get sick, they are the ones I call. They know my children and the other intimate details of my life. They have my personal number and can reach me outside of office hours. They are my friends. We have a relationship. So, for them to ask for the details about my hair is not a fulfillment of their curiosity; it is another exchange in a relational moment. Relationship matters.

We appreciate your appreciation. A compliment, "I like your hair," will suffice. We understand the admiration—we admire each other's hairstyles all the time without the need to ask about the details. Our hair is a place of honor. We ask that you respect the space and, in other words, please do not touch our hair.

Admire It, Don't Touch It,

The Sistahs

About Our Hair

40% of the total survey respondents had responses pertaining to their hair. Of those, 70% commented about the inappropriateness of others touching their hair. **This cannot be overstated, to all my sisters, do not touch a Black woman's hair!**

Dear Sister,
Here's what Black women want you to know . . .

. . . About My Feelings

The fact that the adult American Negro female
emerges a formidable character
is often met with amazement, distaste and even belligerence.
It is seldom accepted as an inevitable outcome
of the struggle won by survivors
and deserves respect if not enthusiastic acceptance.

—Dr. Maya Angelou
American poet, storyteller, activist, and autobiographer

Dear Sister,

As human beings, we experience a variety of feelings. The emotional wheel developed by Dr. Robert Plutchik proposes that people have eight foundational emotions: joy, sadness, trust, disgust, surprise, anticipation, fear, and wait for it…don't forget about the last one…ANGER! That's right, anger is a fundamental human emotion. And while I have plenty to be angry about, I'm not an Angry Black woman! There is a difference.

In ninth grade, I sat in my freshman English class and read the classic novel *The Adventures of Huckleberry Finn* by Mark Twain. Throughout the out-loud reading of the book, my all-white classmates had the opportunity to identify "Nigger Jim" as it was written on the pages. Not "N-word Jim," not "Black Man Jim," not "Jim." But I, the only Black girl in a classroom of twenty-eight other White students, sat through weeks of reading and discussion regarding the vile word used for centuries to denigrate and humiliate my ancestors. And if that wasn't shocking and angering enough, the protest that would ensue from irate parents and students was met with justifications that mirrored the sentiment of it not being that big of a deal. It's just a word.

In 2006, new to Decatur, Georgia, I was attending graduate school and working full-time. I needed childcare for three children, all under the age of five. I went to a childcare center that was in the area, and I walked in with my little ladies—all with long pigtails and cute matching outfits. I asked the lady at the front desk for information regarding their rates for two four-year-olds and a two-year-old. I gasped when she informed me that it would cost $750 per week! The only explanation I could give for her next question was that the deafening pause in the conversation was too much for her to withstand. She met my silence with, "Can you get help from their fathers?" Their fathers? What would make you think they have more than one father? And not that it was any of her business, but my children, all three of them, have one father—a man I married. And if they did, what would give her license to ask such a question? After formulating some words, I found the emotional gravitas to correct her. "Ma'am, my children have one father. And our income, like a lot of people, is not enough to cover the cost of full-time daycare at $750 per week." I gathered my girls and my things and headed for the door. As I was leaving, I heard her say, "Sorry. It was just a mistake."

Some coworkers have more space for socializing outside of work than others. It was the third time this coworker had asked me to bring my kids to his lake house to cook out and sail on the lake with his wife. He told me the rest of the team had been to his house several times, and all the kids had a great time. I was the only teammate that hadn't been. I told him for the third time that I appreciated the invitation, but with how my schedule was set up, I wasn't sure this would happen any time soon. I will never forget when he looked at me and said, "You need to make time for your kids. They grow up so fast." While I didn't owe him an explanation, I was tired of the assumption that because I didn't want to spend my social time with him, that meant I was neglecting time with my kids. I took the next several minutes to rattle off the afterschool schedule that a single mother of three undertakes when all the kids are in activities and none of them are driving. I elaborated on the work I do on Saturdays and the hours of Lyft I drive at night to pay for said activities while he's out on his boat. When I got quiet, there was no apology for the assumption. No regard for what life looks like at my house. No acknowledgment of his ignorance. His only statement was, "Well, that's just my opinion."

Just a word. Just a mistake. Just an opinion. These "just" offenses from society are what we call microaggressions. *Microaggressions*, a term credited to Dr. Chester M. Pierce of Harvard University in the 1970s, are everyday insults, indignities, and demeaning messages sent to people of color by sometimes well-intentioned White people who are unaware of the hidden messages being sent to them.[6] I've heard it said that microaggressions are like paper cuts. They look like the smallest cut, still burn, take forever to heal, and can grow bigger if they continue to be met with friction. Paper cuts hurt! They can make you angry. And society is full of them for Black women.

By the time I was thirty-five, I was resentful, frustrated, and angry. Resentful at the assumptions. Frustrated by the paper cuts. Angry at the many injustices and insults I faced that were considered small happenings that I should overlook as inconsequential. Listening to the word "nigger" in class. My well-meaning White dance teacher who did not understand why I could not change my hair from a ponytail, to straight down, to a French braid backstage between dance numbers. Being followed around stores and watched carefully when I picked something up. Sitting in criminal justice classes, listening to the now-disapproved theories about Black men being dangerous and animalistic. Teachers assumed I was alone and poor because I was single and working hard. And coworkers who felt that because they didn't see my parenting skills, I must not have them. As the list of offenses grew, so did my anger. And no matter how often society tries to tell us that we cannot be angry or hurt, the Bible tells us something else.

As a Jesus follower, how I behave is influenced by how Jesus behaved. Jesus's sayings, behavior, character, and purpose for coming is captured in the four Gospels of the New Testament. Each Gospel is told from a different vantage point. Whether you're reading Matthew's Gospel and focusing on Jesus, the Jewish Messiah, or Mark's Gospel and learning about the suffering Son of God, or reading from Luke's account emphasizing Jesus as the Savior of the World, or learning from John's emphasis of Jesus as the divine Son of God, all of these Gospels help us understand that Jesus got angry!

Jesus was fully divine and fully human, inseparably both, and showed the full range of emotions. There were times when Jesus got angry. In the three Synoptic Gospels (Matthew, Mark, and Luke), the Pharisees were always looking for a way to think the worst of Jesus, even though he was doing good for the people.[7] One day, Jesus went to the synagogue and there was a man with a withered hand. The Pharisees asked Jesus if it was lawful to heal this man even though it was the Sabbath—a day they were not supposed to work. They weren't so much interested in whether to heal the man, but in finding a way to accuse and discredit Jesus. Jesus turns the tables on them by asking them one question that cast doubt on their own intelligence. Jesus' tone in Matthew 12, Mark 3, and Luke 6 was short and forceful with the people that tried to disregard this man with the withered hand. Jesus gets angry when we disregard people's needs.

In Matthew 16, Jesus tells the disciples how his life would end. Peter, one of his closest friends, no doubt meaning well, takes Jesus to the side, and the Bible says Peter rebukes Jesus. If we understand anything about Peter's personality, we know he probably wasn't quiet about it either. Peter was known for his direct and sometimes abrasive communication style. I can picture him almost yelling at Jesus, saying, "God forbid it, Lord! This must never happen to you" (Matthew 16:22, NRSV). And to remind Peter about his greater mission, Jesus matches Peter's energy. Jesus rebukes Peter and calls him a stumbling block. Jesus gets angry when even well-meaning friends get in the way of his bigger purpose.

We see Jesus angry in all four Gospels at what is happening in the Temple, but John's Gospel emphasized the event like this:

> 13It was nearly time for the Jewish Passover celebration, so Jesus went to Jerusalem. 14In the Temple area he saw merchants selling cattle, sheep, and doves for sacrifices; he also saw dealers at tables exchanging foreign money. 15Jesus made a whip from some ropes and chased them all out of the Temple. He drove out the sheep and cattle, scattered the money changers' coins over the floor, and turned over their tables. 16Then, going over to the people who sold doves, he told them, "Get these things out of here. Stop turning my Father's house into a marketplace!" (John 2:13–16, NLT)

The Temple of Jerusalem was a central place in Jewish culture during that time. It was a place of worship, but it was also a place used for judicial and legal matters, buying and selling goods, and having feasts and community events. These interactions were normative. Jesus wasn't upset about them doing community business, he was upset about them mistreating people in the process, more specifically, Jesus was angry over vulnerable people being extorted for money. As a matter of fact, of the few times Jesus got angry was when a person was hurting or mistreating someone else. Jesus gets angry at injustice!

If Jesus showed anger, can we agree that it's okay if we show it too? If not, what emotion does one expect to elicit from people who have spent a lifetime being called out of their name, negatively stereotyped, and robbed of their culture and heritage?[8] What would be the proper emotional response? Anger is often attributed to Black women who refuse to be sweet in the face of oppressive action. But if Jesus can show anger in the face of injustice, shouldn't we be allowed to do the same, and, as Jesus's followers, should it maybe even be expected of us?

America has given countless reasons for Black women to be angry. We are angry at the level of injustice we see and experience. We are tired of having to worry about our sons when they leave the house and having our daughters oversexualized in the media. It demeans our authenticity when we have to change the pitch of our voices to deal with microaggressions at work. It is dehumanizing to be told by strangers, "You should smile; aren't you happy?" as if we are not allowed to experience any other emotion. At times, we are angered by the boxes America has tried to push us into and the oppression we experience. However, experiencing an emotion does not equate to the entirety of who someone is.

More often than not, I do not wake up angry. I wake up determined and thankful for another opportunity to fulfill my purpose, spend time with my kids, and live out my dreams. I sing while I fix coffee. When no one else is in the car with me, I'm laughing out loud, thinking about a conversation I had the day before. And my mind might even drift off to what I have planned that night or weekend. Black women do not walk around angry, but if we did, can you understand how our daily interactions might contribute to that? Can you be sensitive to the paper cuts, the microaggressions, or outright injustices we continue to sustain and never have a chance to heal? Are Black women allowed to have feelings?

Sisters, what do you think about when you hear the phrase "angry?" Do you ever wonder what happened to that person for them to feel that way? You may take the time to consider that our anger is part of our response to centuries of other emotions that we have not been safe enough to express. We've been forced to hold in the grief and shame. We have not had safe spaces to process sadness or loss. Beneath the surface of those of us that are angry are generations of unprocessed trauma. When that emotion is connected to a person, do you ever think they might have the right to be angry? And if they have the right to feel that way, does that necessarily mean their whole being has to be characterized with that one adjective?

Please consider this with me. America has given countless reasons for Black women to be angry. I'd venture to say that the majority of us are not. We feel anger. We get angered. But we are not angry! There is a difference. Putting the adjective before the noun, before the person, means you are judging her feelings before her being, her reaction before her humanity. Black women are wives, moms, leaders, and humans. We feel joy, sadness, enthusiasm, frustration, hope, and despair. I'm not an Angry Black Woman, although there are times when I might be a Black woman who is angry. And like any other human, don't I have the right to feel that emotion too?

Hoping You Feel Me and Will Learn to Allow Me to Feel,

Your Sistahs

About Our Feelings

You don't have to prove pain the way we too often do.

Defending ourselves is not "attacking" you.

No! We are not angry Black women.

I'm hurt and disappointed that society has not arrived at a place where Black women can share our hearts safely, openly, and comfortably about the difficulty of our experiences.

When we have discussions about injustices toward Black people, please understand my sense of urgency fuels my passion.

Don't weaponize your White tears.

Do not mistake my passion for anger.

We respond well to respect.

We are very independent. We love to have engaging conversations. We are not mean.

The term "strong black woman" doesn't mean we should have to deal or put up with anything and everything because we'll get through it. Yes, we have a fighting spirit, but it needs to be nurtured, cared for, and understood too.

All Black women are not loud and angry all the time.

Nursing researchers at New York University and Columbia University found that **Black women are more likely to report self-criticism, self-blame, trouble sleeping, an inability to experience pleasure, and irritability** than the more widely recognized symptoms of depression, like feeling sad or hopeless.

(Jillian Wilson, "Depression Symptoms May Look Different for Black Women. Here's How.," *HuffPost*, January 12, 2023.)

Dear Sister,
Here's what Black women want you to know . . .

. . . *About My Strength*

I am no longer accepting the things I cannot change.
I am changing the things I cannot accept.

—Dr. Angela Y. Davis
Distinguished Professor Emerita
University of California, Santa Cruz
Political Activist

Dear Sister,

No one gets stronger without picking up more weight. But any fitness coach will tell you that everybody needs time for the body to recover from the weight they've been carrying. Here's my concern: when do Black women get to stop carrying the weight that continues to make us appear so strong? When do we get the opportunity to recover?

"You're such a strong Black woman!" I know, you mean that as a compliment. After all, this world often tramples on the weak. But what if I told you that what may seem like a compliment to you is actually a trap that is killing us? What if I told you we are strong because of the unjust weight we've had to carry, and we deserve to put it down? What if I told you our strength is often the excuse companies use to work us harder and pay us less? What if I told you that "strong" is not a compliment? It's a trap! An out for everyone else and a reason to put more on us. And we need you to help us by refusing to continue to put this label on us.

Simone Biles. Naomi Osaka. Sha'Carri Richardson. Three different women with a lot in common. All of these women are decorated professional athletes. All of these women needed a moment to pull back from their careers and exercise self-care. All of these women are Black. And every single one of them was criticized and demonized in the media for not being able to push through and work for the success of their sport, their team, and America's athletic reputation on international stages. These women had already made significant contributions to the world of sports. They had made millions of dollars for corporate sponsors. And as they dealt with health challenges, anxiety, and depression, the world drug them for filth for being human!

In 2017, I moved from Phoenix, Arizona to Charlotte, North Carolina. I was so excited about the new season that lay ahead of me, but I was also trying to put my life back together from a season that had almost destroyed me. Shortly after moving to Charlotte, I had lunch with a new colleague. These lunches were regular occurrences as I was working to build community in an unfamiliar space. During this "I want to get to know you" session, I answered all the usual questions. Where are you from? Tell me about your kids. How did you wind up in ministry? How are you liking Charlotte? And then, in a space that felt especially safe, I began to share what life was really like for me.

I shared the sprinting pace that was demanded of me when I moved to Atlanta to complete my master's degree while working full-time, being a high-capacity volunteer at church, and raising three young girls. I talked about being confident in my call to ministry, but knowing firsthand the level of rejection that comes with being a woman in a male-dominated profession. I talked about having a husband that decided he didn't want to be married and the shame of having people ask me what I did wrong. And we discussed the work it took to pursue a pastoral call while being a single mother raising three daughters in a new city.

As we got back in her car and headed back to the church, she asked me, "What do you do to take care of yourself?" Well, that list was shorter. I take a nap when I get home from work. I eat ice cream probably more than I should. I treat myself to Starbucks on a regular basis. I pray. And worship. A LOT! As a member of a privileged class that has the option to prioritize self-care, she said, "But do you ever just take time to break?"

BREAK! Is she serious? I looked at her and I said, "Who picks up the pieces of my life while I'm breaking?" And that's when it dawned on her. When she breaks, her husband picks up the pieces. Her nanny gives her a break. Or her community, who has the bandwidth in their own lives so they can be there for her, provides that opportunity. I don't have the privilege of a mental breakdown. I get up and go to work, depressed, anxious, and emotionally depleted, regardless, because Black women, especially those of us building professional careers, do not have the privilege to break. We only get the burden of being strong!

The "strong" expectation was applied to us when we exited the slave ships. Gender was rarely considered in the forced labor of enslaved African men and women. The strength differences that are often inherited with gender were disregarded. As Black women came of child-bearing age and were impregnated voluntarily or through rape, the workload didn't change much. Thanks to the work of John Campbell regarding one of the largest plantations in Georgia during the mid-1800s, we know that enslaved Black women only got an average of 24.6 days off to tend to the physical needs of pregnancy and delivery, which lasts an average of 270 days.[9] You can bet the threat of the overseer's whip forcing her to work through sickness, pain, and an enlarged belly required an inordinate amount of physical and emotional strength. And lest we forget the strength required of abolitionist ancestors such as Frances E. W. Harper, Sojourner Truth, Harriet Tubman, and Elizabeth Freeman, just to name a few. We were reaching down and pulling up the strength that it took to just survive and provide opportunities for others to do the same.

It would give me some solace to be able to tell you that Campbell's research was limited to one plantation and not a systemic disregard for the human limitations of our bodies but that would be lie. This stereotype of strength is responsible for the dismissal of pain in Black women for centuries. Since the 1840s when gynecologist J. Marion Sims used our bodies for gynecology experiments, our reproductive organs have never been seen as fragile as other races of women. The dangerousness of childbearing for Black women hasn't changed, as we are still three times more likely to die in childbirth than White women.

We know that it was illegal for Black women to stay at home, so after my elders spent all day taking care of other people's children, cleaning their houses, and cooking their meals, they went home to do much of the same. During the Civil Rights Movement, we marched in heels and stockings, were beaten with nightsticks, and bitten by dogs too, all the while having the mental awareness that we would never be given the same amount of acknowledgment as men even though we were just as involved and did the legwork to make the Movement happen. We were mentally strong enough to withstand the disparity between work and appreciation.

Professionally, we've been strong enough to outpace the majority of other groups in establishing businesses, getting degrees, and building new generational wealth, all while overcoming the disparities that society continues to impose and the stereotypes they uphold. We get why everyone thinks we're so strong. The fact that we are doesn't negate the reality that we shouldn't have to be.

The idea of the "Strong Black Woman" is both factual and mythological. Factually, Black women are often physically and emotionally strong. We've had to be. It is mythological because too many people think our strength negates the reality that we have the same limitations as everyone else. The myth is that we are so strong that we don't feel or get tired. The fact is that those sentiments are lies! Yes, we are strong. And we feel. And we get tired. This myth is upheld by historical precedent and cultural expectations from men and women and people of all races. The fact is that Black women will hold it together. We always have, so it is expected that we always will. The myth is that it doesn't hurt us to do so when the fact is, it is really quite painful. These myths paint us as superhuman. These expectations are robbing us of the reality that we are not.

Do me a favor. Sisters, take a second and think through all the Black women that you know and ask yourself the following questions:

1. Have I ever thought, "She's so strong," or "She's such a strong Black woman"?
2. Do I put the weight of my justice journey on her instead of carrying it myself?
3. Do I look the other way when she carries more than the rest of the team?

If you answered yes to any of these questions, we, the Sistahs, need you to realize how dangerous these thoughts and actions are. Your Black Sisters need you to recognize that we are just as human as you. We need rest at the end of the day, just like you. We need emotional space to be ourselves without having to defend our entire race. We need the space to freely say no to additional projects without being told we're not team players. We want you to acknowledge that being strong is not a privilege; having the space to be human enough to be vulnerable is. We want you to see that we are tired of carrying the weight of society on our shoulders and then being further penalized for being able to do so.

If you want to give your Sisters the protection that history has denied us, you'll pick up some of this weight yourself so that we don't have to keep carrying the fight for justice on our own. Sister, we know that most of you can carry more than you've been conditioned to. And in you carrying more, you give us space to put some of what we're carrying down.

Putting Down the Weight,

The Sistahs

About Our Strength

Strength is not a favored attribute w**hen it is used as a weapon in order to keep us struggling for equality.**

Dear Sister,

Here's what Black women want you to know . . .

. . . About My Career

Even as a professional in an integrated world,
I had been the only black woman
in enough drawing rooms and boardrooms
to have an inkling of the chutzpah it took
for an African American woman
in a segregated southern workplace
to tell her bosses she was sure
her calculations would put a man on the Moon.

—Katherine Johnson
NASA Mathematician

Dear Sister,

Education. Professional success. Financial acumen. All of these things are earned. We've received nothing for free. And we've beaten all the odds to attain it. Black women are professionals too. And we want you to value the journey that it has taken for many of us to get there.

Run faster, jump higher. You have to be twice as good to get half as much. Study more, test better. I heard these lessons explicitly, learned them implicitly, and the heaviness of being a double minority is real. I grew up hearing about the inequality of the workforce for Black women my whole life. Did you know that Black women earn degrees at a rate higher than almost every other demographic? While we make up only 12.7% of the population, we earn undergraduate degrees at a higher rate than every population except White men.[10] Even with this, Black women, on average, still make about 20% less than White women.[11] And when it comes to White men, Black women make $.68 cents for every $1 they make. The way these stats are set up, it seems outworking has not resolved unequal treatment. So then, if it's not education, and it's not a lack of qualification, why is this happening?

Unfortunately, education and qualifications are not always the measuring sticks for promotion and opportunity. Too often, the old adage is true. It's not what you know, but who you know that dictates your next opportunity. And since we're being honest, let me add that it's not just what you know or who you know, but also HOW well you fit in with them that brings about the promotion. What you know…check! Black women have degrees and experience. Who you know…well, that can be a little trickier. Who you know comes down to proximity. And when the majority of people in executive positions are White men, well, proximity for Black women can be challenging. Even with that, my Sistahs have found numerous ways to overcome this hurdle through projects, internships, externships, and creatively building relational equity. But that "how" hurdle is a trip. Pun intended! The "how well you fit in with them" comes down to one word that has become more and more popular over this last generation of professionals and is a breeding ground for biases to prevent equality. And that word is CULTURE!

Have you ever been blindsided at work? I have. I had been on the job for almost two years. The honeymoon phase had been over for a while, but I still thought things were going pretty well. I had helped with several significant projects that would increase the organization's ability to serve the community. Administrative efficiency is one of my greatest strengths, so I put that to work doing things I thought would save the organization time and money. In addition to taking on this extra workload, I started new programs that would serve the underprivileged in the city and increase the organization's visibility. I thought it was in line with the organization's goal of growing diversity. While I had made only a few deep connections with people on my team, I felt the dynamics were still professional and sometimes even jovial. I figured I was getting along with most everyone, and no one could argue with the value that I was adding to the team.

Then it happened. Every other Wednesday, I had a standing meeting with one of my supervisors. Our relationship had hit a rocky spot, but nothing could have prepared me for the discussion that was about to happen. Like every other meeting, I sent him my discussion guide the night before. I went into his office prepared to discuss projects I was working on and the tasks that I had completed. While I was going through my list, I felt like something was off. Have you ever been in a conversation with someone, and the positive energy you are giving is not the energy that is being reciprocated? Yeah, it was kind of like that. The conversation took such a swift turn that I do not even remember how it got there. But it is a destination many Black women have visited.

The conversation came down to what he defined as "culture." Even though I went to more lunches and coffees than ever, I wasn't friendly or relational enough. Even though I never said no to projects and struggled to get what I needed for my own, I was seen as unapproachable. Even though I never yelled in a meeting, a coworker characterized me as aggressive. As the bi-weekly conversation went on, I finally heard the one subjective sentence that Black professional women hear too often: "You're just not fitting into the culture."

Performance…check. Productivity…check. Contribution… yep…I was doing that too. But I was being penalized because my coworkers couldn't relate to me regardless of how much I bent to relate to them.

Culture is a loaded word. But let me remind you of how I'm using it. Culture is about how one shows up in the world. It influences how we interpret other people's actions. Our experiences influence our cultural outlook. People have individual cultural outlooks. Families have cultures and interpret actions differently from other people down the street. And organizations, regardless of what is written, have cultures too! They have ways in which they interpret the introvert who doesn't do well in coworking spaces. They have ways in which they interpret the tone in someone's voice. Organizations have embedded, and often unspoken, value systems on relationships versus performance. In a world where Black women have only recently been accepted at executive levels, we're asked to fit into a culture we didn't create and that, too often, we're being hired to help change.

The truth is, like so many other Black women, I was a diversity hire. I was hired to bring more diversity to an organization that was fine with embracing different colors of people but had not yet done the internal work to embrace different cultures of people. Organizations that really want different cultures, and not just different colors, embrace different work styles. When an organization wants to diversify cultures, they look for the benefit of different communication styles. And when a corporation values diversity more than homogeneity, they counter the inherent bias that comes with subjective feedback by focusing more on objective measures. When this is not the case, Black women rarely thrive as diversity hires because once we become part of the organization, the goalpost moves from diversification to assimilation.

Assimilation, too often, is the name of the game for Black women in predominantly White professional spaces. And assimilation hurts! Assimilation for Black women requires taking our multidimensional selves and allowing people to cut away at us until they only have to see the parts they can handle without ever having to adjust their own vision. It slowly kills who we are so that we can fit into whatever caricature the organization wants us to be. Assimilation erases the image of God that is present in me to create a person in the image of the company.

Sisters, while the majority of executive level seats are still designated to White men, we need you to know that you have some responsibility here. The highest hurdle we face in the race to professional equality is getting people to see past their own cultural preferences to recognize our contributions.

This may look like laying down your preoccupation with being friends for our need to maintain a boundary of emotional safety. Is it really necessary for a coworker to go to lunch with you? Is it necessary to "like someone in order to work with someone?" Can you respect their work ethic and production without being invited into their personal space?

This may look like taking our feedback at face value instead of trying to interpret it through a tone of speech or pitch of voice. Tone of voice is something that is taught. It is cultural. Tone-policing is when you refuse to hear what someone says because you may not like the way they said it. But I want you to consider this: the truth is the truth no matter who tells it! If the completed project misses all the objectives, regardless of the tone of my speech, it's not good! If you say something inaccurate, the pitch of the voice giving the feedback doesn't change its accuracy. When tone is the hurdle for receptivity, bias is at play.

Professional equality might include refusing to accept complaints about us that only have subjective statements without objective measures. If diversity matters, if we value all people, we have to get clarification when someone uses a word like "aggressive" to describe another person. What do you mean by aggressive? Did they throw something? Did they call you a name? Did they threaten you? These are objective measures for an aggressive accusation. What about that person makes you feel they are aggressive? These questions push the hearer to take responsibility for their perception and make sure there is a factual measure that lies outside their cultural framework.

Taking responsibility for professional equality and organizational diversity may include holding staff members accountable for racially inappropriate actions or words instead of defending their actions to us by stories of your relationships with them. It really doesn't matter how long you've known them. Or if you think their intentions weren't bad. If their words or actions were harmful, then we need you to recognize the impact.

Sisters, should your Black Sisters have to continue to jump hurdles of prejudice and bias when our performance has already cleared them? Removing the hurdle means giving us more than the benefit of the doubt. It means judging us on the content of our character and the production of our work instead of the nuances of our culture.

Black women continue to work too hard to be tripped up by biases erected to protect privilege. Our personalities should not have to be torn apart from our capabilities, and it's time for the world to value both and compensate us accordingly.

Whole Professionals,

The Sistahs

About Our Careers

Black women not only deserve a seat at the table, but we earned it. We didn't get to our success because we are fulfilling a quota, a diversity stat, etc. Stop questioning our personal and professional success. Just celebrate it!

We deserve to earn the same wages as everyone else. We've earned it.

Statements such as "you speak good English" are offensive.

We are not "trying" or "acting" White if we are, and thus sound, educated. It is rude to say "You don't sound Black."

Please don't act surprised when you find out I am a lawyer. It's 2023! Black people are successful.

Accents and regional dialects are not indicators of intelligence or the lack thereof.

We're tired of putting in 10-times the amount of effort to get a fraction of the recognition.

When you say "You are so articulate," what I just heard is that you expected me not to be.

We are statistically more educated, more experienced, better equipped, and more dedicated to getting the job done than most. And we are rewarded for this by being given more work for less pay than our counterparts.

Don't ask me why I speak so properly!

While statistically we know that Black women have more advanced degrees than every demographic other than White men, **one-third of Black women who answered this survey made statements about being underappreciated and undercompensated** for their educational achievements and professional contributions.

Dear Sister,
Here's what Black women want you to know . . .

. . . About Our Unity

*Women, if the soul of the nation is to be saved, I be-
lieve that you must become its soul.*

—Mrs. Coretta Scott King
Civil Rights Activist
Architect of the Legacy of Dr. Martin Luther King, Jr.

Dear Sister,

When the Sistahs call for unity, our voice kind of shakes. Not because we don't want it, but because Black women and White women often say the same word with two very different definitions. When we say unity, we're asking for practices that value us. When you say unity, too often it is for practices that ask us to lay down the parts of ourselves we value. When we say unity, we're asking for you to fight for us. Experience teaches us that when White women have asked us to join with them in unity, we've been asked to stop fighting for ourselves. Too often unity comes at our expense. If we have to lessen ourselves to get you to value us, then it is not unity. It is erasure.

When we call for unity, it is usually interpreted as "help us be like you"—help us change our tone, straighten our hair, accept your political priorities, and even worship God in the manner that White people deem appropriate. But when we are calling for unity, we are not crying out to lay down who we are. We are not volunteering to deny our hurdles or ignore our hurts. We are not offering to ignore our culture or even to be willing to share it with people who don't understand the cost it took to establish it. When we say unity, we are calling for you, the Sisters, to empathize with our hurts and fight to heal these wounds. Our unity looks like loving us more than the power that makes your preferences normal and treats our humanity as questionable.

Unity is not real if it demands assimilation to the power that has oppressed us for so long. Unity pushes for policies that protect people from harm and looks for ways to speak out against practices that result in disparities. It looks for solutions to dismantle oppression before asking the oppressed what they did wrong. Real unity is a byproduct of love that is powerful enough to undo unjust systems.

Love can be a deceptive word, especially in American culture. It seems to be thrown around in whimsical ways. We use it in referencing our favorite sports team, a personality on social media, and every Tuesday when it comes time for tacos. I mean, I get it, who doesn't love a Taco Tuesday? But we've fallen in love with the word love. It gives us warm fuzzies and connects us to positive energy. But that kind of surface-level application— love without cost—will not produce the unity we need to create a more just world.

The love that produces unity is a love that gives more than it takes, stays when it wants to run, and fights for what is right instead of remaining where it is comfortable. In the words of Dr. Cornel West, "Justice is what love looks like in public." When people are loved enough to be treated justly that will bring about unity. The level of love that results in justice that will bring about unity is nothing short of agape.

Agape is love that is active and alive.[12] It values the image of God in each individual and fights for the protection of their humanity regardless of what it costs in return. It doesn't fade over time. Agape love is like water. It is a life-giving force on its own, but often needs context to give it shape. Paul gives it shape and definition in 1 Corinthians 13:4-8a (NIV) when he says that:

> Love is patient, love is kind. It does not envy,
> it does not boast, it is not proud. It does not
> dishonor others, it is not self-seeking, it is not

easily angered, it keeps no record of wrongs.
Love does not delight in evil but rejoices with
the truth. It always protects, always trusts, always hopes, always perseveres. Love never fails.

Agape will be active enough to overcome the grossness that is racism and is patient in fighting. Agape takes short and slow steps to build relationships with Black women over time instead of demanding trust that has not been earned with action. Agape considers how your actions impact the recipient regardless of your intent, and doesn't require the recipient to accept the action as kind when the impact is harmful. It takes into account the damage that has been done to the Sistahs over time and gives them space to feel hurt, grieve the loss, and mourn over the mis-treatment. It recognizes when it needs to be silent and listen but stands up in unity when it needs to be loud and give voice to the experiences of a population that have gone unheard for far too long. Then it takes action based on what it hears. Love requires action. Love that is just emotion is not love at all.

And trust me when I say, Black women have limited capacity to carry your emotion. Our plates are full, fighting the systems that I've already written about that threaten to tear down our self-worth and zap our energy. We need your actions to match your emotions when you say you are with us. We need you to be with us at the Thanksgiving table by correcting Uncle Bill when he insults Black women and scoffs at policies that support our families. We need you to unify with us in the voting booth when policies that affect our health and prenatal care are on the ballot. We need you to vote like you care about the life of the Sistahs just as much as the life of the children we carry. We need you to love the Black child you adopted by learning their needs, their culture, and how to care for their curls and skin. We need your love to protect them and prepare them for the reality they will face as adults where your whiteness can't protect them. Unity requires taking all the emotion in your tears and loving the Sistahs enough to put action behind them.

Unity requires a love that fights for the Sistahs. Because when you love your sister, you fight for your sister. You know this if you have a sister. I had a younger sister, and you can believe nobody came for her unless they came for me. We disagreed on a lot of things. But when her value was threatened, when people said hurtful things, or events happened that threatened her success, I was right there to fight with and for her. I bet I can say the same about you. If a bully was chasing your sister home from school, if you couldn't beat them, at the very least you helped your sister outrun them.

I don't think we can outrun racism. In reality, evil is always down for the chase. We need to beat it. We need to roll up our sleeves and say enough is enough. This is the last generation of Black women you will taunt, torment, and hurt. The Sistahs have been victimized by it, and we need you to use your strength to fight back. That is love in action. And that, over time, will bring unity.

Fighting for Unity with You,

Your Sistahs

About Our Unity

Love your neighbor as yourself, regardless of race, creed, or color.

You can build trust by being an active ally, defending Black lives daily, listening when I talk, showing empathy, assuming you don't know, and remembering you're not the authority.

I would like to have real, authentic relationships with White women and White people, but you need to understand that when you are oblivious to your own ingrained cultural racism, it makes it hard. If you are not aware of your own biases, you will mistreat Black people in word, gesture, and/or spirit without even knowing it.

Be intentional about spending time with a diverse group of friends and be sincere.

We are going to have different perspectives in the way we view the world and that should be okay.

Invalidating my oppression means you're siding with the oppressor.

We are not your competition. We are not the enemy.

You cannot produce Black babies and still be neutral about the injustice against Black bodies.

In my relationship with Christ, I believe that He is calling me to remain open to authentic relationships with White people despite all the issues that divide us. Know that I am praying for you and our community whether you are my sister in Christ or not.

It's okay to help us…whatever that means to you. At the grocery store, in the gym, with law enforcement, as neighbors, etc.

Unity cannot come at the expense of the Black woman's ability to bring her whole self to the table. **True unity welcomes the best part of all people in order to make a better society as a whole.**

For My Sistahs

*Sometimes you see how humanity can rise above
any kind of cultural ills and hate
that a person's capacity to love and communicate
and forgive can be bigger than anything else.*

—Viola Davis
EGOT Winning Actress

To My Sistahs,

There was no way I would close this out without addressing a letter to you. It is true, this book is to help other women
understand what we want them to know. But for this last letter,
there are some things I want to share from my heart to yours.
So consider this a letter entitled *Dear Sistah: There's Something
Your Sistah Wants You to Know.*

The work of Dear Sister is largely possible because you were
willing to recount experiences that are othering, hurtful, and frus-
trating for the betterment of our communities. I know that it cost
you more than time to put down your remarks. Remembering
hurtful comments and painful experiences opens up old wounds
that we like to move on from and often need to repress in order
just to survive. Your vulnerability has made this work doable, and
it is my goal that it will help other women become more like our
Sisters than our enemies.

I have laid out the case in the previous pages on how history
has served to erect social constructs and systemic barriers that
make it difficult for us to live out our purpose. Don't get me
wrong, we have and will continue to succeed. That's that *Black
Girl Magic*! But these constructs and barriers are killing us physically, affecting us financially, and inhibiting us psychologically.

These constructs contribute to our high rates of hypertension
and diabetes. The stress we suffer affects the frequency of fibroids amongst us, the high rate of infertility and infant mortality

in our community, and even the rate of obesity. These barriers make our road toward purpose and professional achievement stonier. It short-circuits our careers. The standards of beauty that we're pushing against cost us financially, cause us psychological damage, and create in-fighting from Sistah-to-Sistah. The mental health field is just starting to take our challenges seriously and recognizing that they cannot diagnose our needs with the same measures they use for White men. Racism sucks, and it is trying to suck the life out of us, but it is for these very unfortunate reasons we are most equipped and must lead this work even though we didn't ask for the job.

And while we continue to fight the principalities of racism and patriarchy, we must remember that we don't do it from the start line. We stand on the shoulders of generations of ancestors and elders that have sacrificed an incalculable amount for this work. We understand the power of the village more than most and the necessity of continuing to walk the trails that have been blazed before us. I honor the mothers of the justice movement that have been quoted and named throughout this book, but I also hold close the many others that weren't named and the spirits of those we will never be able to call. It is this cloud of witnesses that pushed me to type through tears and frustration to completion.

The sacrifice of our elders should compel us to continue in what sometimes seems like an impossible work, the work of justice in a world that insists on treating us unjustly. The same way our ancestors and elders thought about us, we must think about the Black girls that will come after us. We cannot be so tired of trying that we selfishly give up. We cannot be so disenchanted with the dream of better that we resign ourselves to "good enough." Justice for our descendants requires that we continue to work for justice now. And even if we don't see the future that we are fighting for, we deserve the best this world has to offer us while we are here. We, you, my Sistah, are worth the fight. Resignation to less than is not an option.

Now while we are most qualified to lead others out of their blindness of supremacy, let's hold space for our Sistahs that are not in a place to do this work right now. In our collective resistance, we must be able to block for our Sistahs that are too frustrated, angry, or wounded to have these conversations and step into these spaces. To you, I say, "Sis, go do what you gotta do!" We want you with us. We need you with us. But I recognize that, for some us, helping others is coming at the cost of our own demise. In the words of one of the people I continue to do this work with, take a walk but do not walk away. Go for a minute. Go find your safe space. Find a therapist of color that can understand your frustrations. Reignite your faith within an African American community, so they can remind you that you are created in the image of and loved by the One who is Divine. Erect boundaries of relational safety with people that you don't have to explain yourself to. Give your voice and your fight a time to rest and recuperate. But we hope you come back to join us. Heavy work is made lighter by more hands.

While there is a group of us that may need to take a walk, I believe that some of us know we have to get in the fight but are not sure where to jump in. Jumping into this fight for justice requires an honest look within ourselves. Have we adopted thoughts and ideas that perpetuate self-hatred? Do you have trouble accepting your own skin tone? When you look in the mirror, do you talk badly about your own curl pattern? Have you started to believe the stereotypes that the media pushes across our screens? If so, I'd say that your work starts with you. No matter what anyone says, please read this and hear my heart: you were made in the image of God. There is nothing inferior about who you are. Our community is not inherently inferior to anybody else's. As a matter of fact, you are the descendant of a long lineage of kings, queens, and great people who have formed the world with their very hands. You are phenomenal! You are great!

Greatness comes with responsibility even when that greatness is hated by others. You have a responsibility to love yourself and then allow that love to flow to other people. Sometimes that love looks like correcting lies and stereotypes. It may look like speaking out in a meeting where you are more comfortable with being silent. It looks like showing patience with people that simply do not know any better and being forgiving to people who are too ignorant to care. Greatness means we love when others are unloving to us. It means answering slow movement with a consistent push towards progress. Greatness means rejecting the desire to settle for the status quo. We have come a long way from the slave ships and we have miles to go before we sleep. Our job is to make sure that we nor the world around us stops moving along those miles!

There's also a third group of us in the fight and ready to lead us to the next plateau. The movement for justice is not dead. Your fight gives us strength to forge ahead. For my Sistahs in the front, nationally or in your communities, thank you for your pressing. We honor you for your pushing. But from one area leader to another, please make sure you take time to care for you. To rejuvenate yourself. To strengthen your resolve. To continue to massage your heart. Fighting for justice has a way of incessantly planting bitterness in the hearts of those who do it. Guard against it! A bitter heart cannot extend love to those who continue to hurt others and hope to show them that there is a better way.

We must continue to fight for justice to help those who are blind to the reality that their oppression of another human being is a reflection of their own dead nature. I understand that some of you may think it is not your responsibility to help others see the injustices they perpetuate. And you are entitled to your opinion. I just happen to think more in line with Dr. Martin Luther King, Jr. on this point in that *"we are caught in an inescapable network of mutuality, tied in a single garment of destiny. Whatever affects one directly affects all indirectly,"* even if those who have historically benefited from the oppression don't see it.

It is impossible to oppress a group of people without the oppression also killing the perpetrator. One of the reasons I'm so passionate about this work is that I mourn over the loss of humanity that exists for people who insist on treading on others. I am saddened for those who don't understand that if love is defined by 1 Corinthians 13:4-8a, then hate is defined by the antithesis of Paul's description. If love is patient, kind, humble, polite, giving, forgiving, truth-telling, believing, hopeful, and enduring, then hatred is the exact opposite. Too many other demographics define hate using extreme acts of violence. But hate is more subtle than that. Hate is impatient, mean, arrogant, rude, selfish, bitter, deceptive, doubtful, and gives up on people easily. And hatred kills! Our fight for justice includes helping people see where they've been unjust and unloving. But justice is not the ultimate goal. At least not for Jesus' followers. Justice is just a lap in the race toward the work of reconciliation that we are called into. Our goal is to grasp and live out that ministry.

Bridges are never built from one direction. As we call other people into this work of justice and reconciliation, we must stay in it ourselves. We are teaching what we know. Prejudice hurts everybody. Discrimination hides God's beauty. And racism is an ugly systemic evil that, if created by humans (which we know they did), can also be dismantled by humans. Because we have experienced all three, prejudice, discrimination, and racism, we know what it looks like for it not to exist. Let's continue to show the world that picture.

In the Race Against Racism with You,

Your Sistah, Paula Dannielle

One Last Word

Here are nine letters compiled from the feedback of Black women throughout the United States. To my Sistahs, this book would not have been complete without my heartfelt letter to you. This book has been in the works for more than eighteen months and I feel like there is still so much to say. But in reality, I can rewrite these letters several times and it will be impossible to gather all that you need to know. Because American history is so layered, and the journey of Black women so varied, there will always be more to say. There will be more perspectives to learn and other stories to honor. While the research serves as a reliable sample of experiences, and I've done my best to capture my own in this work, take it as learning the experiences from one Black woman as you start or continue the work of learning from other members of my community.

Someone asked me what I want to accomplish with this work. I hope this work does three things.

First, I hope these letters have given you a realistic perspective of some of the things that Black women face on a daily basis. I hope it gives you a peek into our conversations and the hurdles that we have to jump. I hope you could envision the whiplash that is the fight for justice. I hope that you were able to picture my family members. I wanted you to see the days I went to work and struggled to get people to embrace my competence and see my character while they resisted my culture. It was my goal to write with such descriptive detail that you could feel my tears hit the keyboard, see me pacing in-between letters, and hear me questioning if I was giving you too much of my reality. My prayer is that this collection of letters impacted your perspective.

Second, I hope it saves another Black woman from having to relive the pain that I've had to tap into in order to write some of these letters. Have you seen the t-shirts that say "'We Tired' -Black Women"? Well, the sentiment of the shirt is true. We are tired of saying the same thing over and over to one person at a time. I wanted to give my Sistahs some reprieve so I sat out to write what I know many of us are thinking, feeling, and living. To the Black women that will read this book, I hope I captured your experiences faithfully and saved you some conversations.

Third, I hope it continues to pull us closer into a sisterhood that will change the world that we've inherited. I have raised three daughters. They are all young adults and I cringe at the possibility that they may one day decide to have children and my granddaughters will incur some of the same issues as their grand-mother, great-grandmother, and other Black female ancestors. The world that we received is not the world we have to leave, but in order to make that wish a reality, the conversations have to continue.

For the sake of the generations of people coming behind us, we, the Sistahs and Sisters, have to get this right. We have to listen to how we got here, listen to how far we have to go, and then put on our shoes to walk toward healing together. My prayer is that this book contributes to that end.

From Sistah to Sister,

Paula Dannielle

Things to Consider

Reflection Questions "...About Showing Up"

What do I feel in conversations about racism?

How do I show up physically in conversations about racism?

Reflection Questions "...About Our History"

How do you feel when you reflect on America's history of racial oppression? What emotions come up for you?

If someone was writing a history book on what is happening right now racially, what role would you play?

What can you do to create a better future when it comes to race relations in your community?

Reflection Questions "...About My Sistahs"

Has anyone ever assumed something about you that wasn't true?

Identify a few cultural experiences and practices in your life. What are the values of those? How would (or does) it feel for those to not be respected?

**What are some perceptions you hold about Black women?
Does that contribute to how you interact with them?**

Reflection Questions "...About My Family"

Part of this work is doing your own work. This letter gave several examples of children who didn't get to be children. Look up their stories.

Imagine yourself as a child, what would your younger self feel in these situations? Can you imagine how that may have changed how you interact with authority? With Law Enforcement?

Now, imagine a child you care about being treated like the Exonerated Five, Tamir, Shakera, Kiara? What feelings does that bring up for you?

Reflection Questions "...About My Hair"

Have you ever touched a Black woman's hair or asked her questions about her hair? What do you think she was feeling in that moment?

Besides touching a Black woman's hair, are there other boundaries you may be tempted to cross or signs of affection that may actually cross boundaries?

Reflection Questions "...About My Feelings"

Do you think it is okay to be angry? Why or why not? Consider what you have been taught about anger, either spiritually or culturally. Are the scripts you have about anger true?

Think back to a time when you were angry beyond words. Then, I want you to think about what caused that emotion. What else happened that day, week, or month? Who was involved? What were the events surrounding it? Now, what posture can you take to show empathy for your Black sisters who may be having an angry moment?

Reflection Questions "...About My Strength"

When did you last say or think about a Black woman as "strong?" Consider what it may have taken, or is still taking, for her to do what you classify as strong. What sacrifices did she have to make that weren't noticeable at the time or acknowledged by others?

Have you benefited from the "Strong Black Women" in your everyday life? How? Is there something you can do to lighten the load?

Reflection Questions "...About Our Careers"

How does culture show up in your workplace?

When you picture someone qualified, educated, and professional, what does that person look like? How are your definitions of "professional" shaped by culture (or prejudice)?

What are some hurdles Black women may face in your workplace due to cultural differences?

What are some ways you can make your workplace safer for Black women?

Reflection Questions "...About Our Unity"

Reconciliation work often takes an emotional toll, and learning more about racism can come with a lot of emotion. What are some ways Black women are asked to carry their emotions in this work? What are some things you can do instead?

In what ways do we sometimes ask Black women to lay down who they are for the sake of unity? Have you ever seen that or been a part of that?

What are some practical steps you can take to fight for justice and unity?

Reflection Questions "For The Sistahs"

What are some practices you can cultivate to remind yourself of your worthiness and belovedness?

What do you need in order to keep working toward reconciliation?

Who are the people you can go to for support when you need it?

Acknowledgments

When this journey started over two years ago, I had no idea that it would turn into this. I knew that I had something I wanted people to "LIS'N" to but I wouldn't have imagined that I also had something I wanted them to read. I am truly thankful to the people below who pushed me, fought with me, canceled plans on me or allowed me to cancel on them, because they knew the time was now to share what Black women want other women to know. For each of you, I am truly thankful!

Two years ago, you took a chance on a coaching call with me and here's the fruit of your invested time. Thank you for asking me, "What do you want people to listen to?" **Jennifer Barnes**, I am forever grateful for our friendship.

Thank you for fighting for me, pushing me, and making me find the feelings that I was more than comfortable to hide. **Lauren Sellers**, the copyeditor I cannot write without, you are dearly loved.

You invested in my baby girl and now you're supporting me. **Jess Hatmaker**, thank you for your patience with my questions and the expertise of your eye.

To my cover designer, **Sara**, and my interior layout designer, **Bob**, thank you for working with a first-timer and stopping so many of my mistakes.

It's amazing how quickly someone can become family. The occasion of our meeting was one of the most difficult of my life, but I'm eternally grateful for you seeing what was bubbling inside of me. Your hands touched too many parts of this dream for me to name. And yes, **Kimberly Sneed**, tell him that you are my favorite. LOL!

Y'all are the people brave enough to test the food to figure out what's missing. Incredible professionals in your own fields of expertise, **Jumoke**, **Kristyn**, **Ryan**, and **Meagan** thank you for lending your perspectives to the feedback I needed to hear without fear of how I'd feel after hearing it. Your touch is the bow on top of this work.

And to the Black women who gave your voices to the surveys so that we can educate and inspire women around the country, thank you for your honesty, your vulnerability, and saying one more time things that I'm sure you're sick of saying. I hope your sentiments are wholly captured in this work.

To my family and friends that continue to support the work that I do, thank you for all the text messages, encouraging words, and correcting the familial stories. We stand in this work together.

Chayil, **Charity**, **Cherish**, my girls, my CH3, thank you for giving me the space and time to fulfill this next step on my journey. Even as young kids, you all gave me the inspiration I needed to steward every moment the best I could. I hope I inspire you to do the same. Thank you for being generous and loving during this process.

Notes

1. Gil Rendle, *Quietly Courageous: Leading the Church in a Changing World*, (Lanham: Rowman & Littlefield, 2019), 253.

2. Office of Health Equity, *Working Together to Reduce Black Maternal Mortality,* Center for Disease Control, 2022 December 15.

3. Angela Neal-Barnett, PhD. *To Be Female, Anxious and Black,* Anxiety & Depression Association of America, Anxiety and Depression Association of America, 2018 April 23.

4. Stephanie Pappas, *Effective Therapy with Black Women.* American Psychological Association, 2021 November 1.

5. Jo Jones, Ph.D., and William D. Mosher, Ph.D., *Fathers' Involvement With Their Children: United States, 2006–2010,* National Health Statistics, 2013 December 20.

6. Tori DeAngelis, *Unmasking racial microaggressions,* American Psychological Association, February 2009.

7. The term "Synoptic Gospels" refer to Matthew, Mark, and Luke because of their similar stories, wording, and sequence.

8. "Called out of their name" is a colloquialism used when one person refers to another using an obscenity or derogatory phrasing. This can include anything from telling someone "You a lie!" to more harsh terms usually referenced as profanity.

9. John Campbell, *Work, Pregnancy, and Infant Mortality among Southern Slaves,* The Journal of Interdisciplinary History vol. 14: no. 4 (1984), 793–812

10. National Center for Education Statistics, *Degrees Conferred by Race/Ethnicity and Sex*, 2020, June, Table 321.20.

11. Mathilda Roux, *Five Facts about Black Women in the Labor Force,* U.S. Department of Labor, 2021 August.

12. Agape love is one of the types of love found in the New Testament in the original Greek language.